DOWNLOAD THE AUDIOBOOK FREE!

READ THIS FIRST

Just to say thanks for buying my book, I would like
to give you the Audiobook version 100% FREE!

TO DOWNLOAD GO TO:

http://www.thegrowthgurus.co.uk/Goforgrowth/audiobook

The Essential Guide

on how to

Grow your Business

and become

Financially Free

within

3 years

David Hugo Hargreaves

Author: David Hargreaves

Founder and Chief Guru at The Growth Gurus

www.thegrowthgurus co.uk.

"What our readers have had to say"

⋆────❖⚓◦────⋆

"One for the ages, a stand out modern classic in the competitive and vast personal development field. The mix of real life experience combined with the wisdom and knowledge from past and present masters in their field is captivating and very educational. David's honest stripped back story and writing style is a breath of fresh air and is an easy and very enjoyable read, making the content simple to understand and implement. A must read for anyone who wants to better themselves, achieve more, be more, do more and enjoy life at the same time. 5 stars from me'."

Chris Hawthorne. CEO. Changing Space
www.changing-space.co.uk

"Anyone who knows David realises that he has the happy knack of combining his financial and business expertise with clear practical communication which is easy for any businessperson to understand and put into practice, something he has managed to do for a number of Forum of Private Business members over the years and something he has now managed to distil into this book which many small businesses will find invaluable!"

Ian Cass. Managing Director. The Forum of Private Businesses.
www.fpb.org

"My first thought when I came across David's book was, here we go another self help book! What a pleasant surprise when I eventually started reading it! It's a very practical no nonsense approach to running and scaling a business and get your life back type kind of book from someone who's walked the walk, without the bluster that our cousins across the pond can be guilty of! Don't let your ego get in the way of not reading this, there are so many tips and even reminded me of stuff that I knew but had forgotten to apply in my own life!!"

Chris McLeod. CEO. Transparent Windows
www.transparentwindows.co.uk

"David's honest stories give you practical step-by-step guides for all the business owners. He will change your whole mindset about how you structure and run your business. By learning the difference between high and low-value activities will help you to focus where it is necessary. You will get solutions for your problems at any stage where you are at. This is a must-read business book for anyone, who is on the entrepreneurial journey. 5 STARS!"

Sandor Turoczi. CEO. ST Property Solutions
www.stpropertysolutions.org

"Have you ever felt like you have been banging your head on the wall? Well, by the end of the book, the line "look this is how you bloody do it" came to mind and must have been what David was feeling trying to help people escape the 9-5 rat race, because this book is no-nonsense, straight talking and to the point. Easily teaching you how you too could be financially free in less than 3 years with a nice personal touch."

David T. Wade CEO David T. Wade & Co
www.davidtwade.co.uk

"A full to the brim learning experience which I highly recommend to all no matter their interests. This is a refreshingly straight to the point educational and very impressive read which I will revisit often for reference. Top class David."

William Watters CEO Sky Parking Services
skyparkingservices.co.uk

"What they don't teach you on your MBA behavioural science course - this work offers grounded, practical advice for entrepreneurs of all levels. The guidelines presented in the book stand on the shoulders of giants in business development expertise, yet the approaches remain firmly embedded in terra firma in their simplicity of description. A thoroughly enjoyable read that leaves the reader determined to implement many of the suggested strategies."

Anjam Butt MBA CEO
www.hornoempartners.com

"If there was ever a 'tell it like it is' book this is it. It's a down to earth account of what you should be doing right now to ensure your financial future is secure. It's an easy read that will open your eyes to the possibilities you didn't even know existed!"

Alan Jaques CEO Seren Property
www.serenproperty.net

"I've grown tired recently of many of the books being churned out by so called 'experts' and 'gurus' that are simply 'brochures' that have been padded out. So much so that I keep rereading the classics such as Rich Dad Poor Dad and The 'E' Myth. David's book combined both of these amazing books however David's book is far superior on many levels, including being far more practical implementation stuff that's been a significant help to me and my business already."

Heather Watters CEO Inlinked .
www.inlinked.co.uk

Content

1. What is the book all about?

I wrote this book to be your guide to help you become financially independent by growing your business and your wealth beyond your wildest dreams. I am not going to apologise for the primary objectives of this book.

I have a huge dream; to help one million people to become financially independent and to have time freedom.

Building your fortune that can financially sustain you and your family for generations to come is a primary driver in most successful people's lives and is certainly in mine.

Many of the books that you have read already will tend to focus on the 'ideas' of business growth without giving you the tools to implement these ideas. Often these books have not been written by people who have built a successful business. Don't get me wrong; I love books that write about ideas and principles; this book is not that type.

I designed the book to be interactive, and you need to take part to gain the most out of it. As the Lottery slogan goes, 'You've got to be in it to win it.'

At the end of every chapter, I ask you to undertake a task or two. I may also ask you to visit our website and download templates. I will often ask you to involve your colleagues, business partners, coaches, and mentors.

Please take part in all of these exercises because that is the best way to learn and grow. If you are not growing in business, you are going to fail.

Involve others in every step, and this includes your family as well as your colleagues and advisors. You may feel ridiculous at the start, but you will soon learn to embrace the interaction. Reading and implementing this guide to business growth will be far less productive if you alone read it and act on the principles, ideas, systems, and inspirations.

There is no such thing as a self-made man; success takes teams, and as Newton once said. If I have seen further than others, it is by standing on the shoulders of giants.

2. Acknowledgements

Over the last 25 years, I have read hundreds of books on management, business, and self-development. I have benefited from a whole gaggle of mentors, coaches, and advisors and gained massive levels of practical experience by leading the growth of several £ multi-million businesses.

The ideas and principles in this book are, therefore, very seldom my own. It takes a genius to be genuinely original, and I'm not one for reinventing the wheel. That's a high-risk endeavor that I have tried on occasions, and that hardly ever ends well.

During the early stages of building my first business, I owe much to Tony Robbins, Michael E Gerber, Jim Rohn, Dale Carnegie and Zig Zigler, to name but a few.

I also owe thanks to studying people around me who failed to build businesses that operated without their day-to-day input that left them working like dogs. My father was one of these. The minute he stopped working, the income stopped, and that left a mark on my soul that left me horrified of duplicating this business scenario.

I believe that businesses 'winners' have very few original ideas themselves. They put all their knowledge, their own experiences, and the experiences of others, and then they crafted it all together to pass on the wisdom and foresight we all need to succeed. I hope to follow in their footsteps.

I owe a massive level of gratitude to all of the directors I've worked with over the many years. All of whom have helped mold me and mold this book into reality.

I also thank all the business people whom I meet every day who also have, in their way, contributed to this book and, therefore, to your future success. I wrote this book over a period of 3 years, and virtually every week, I have added a little bit more because of their ideas, principles, and insights.

Every day is a school day, and I remind myself of that daily.

After all these years of growing and learning, I continue to be humbled by the world's level of wisdom and knowledge.

Over the last 25 years, my strategy has been to copy closely and then improve the best parts of other people's ideas, other people's businesses, and the teachings of others; successes and failures. The result is that I benefit from literally thousands of years' worth of knowledge and experience to improve the **odds of our success dramatically. It is this vast vessel of knowledge and** experience that I wish now to pass onto you.

I wrote this book to teach you the essentials of building a successful business, building considerable personal wealth while creating and sustaining a happy family and social life. You can then add your learning, experiences and sprinkle in your magic.

Don't believe the 'wannabes' who tell you that you need to hustle 12-14 hours a day, 7 days a week, and sacrifice everything. That's just b*llshit. Business and financial growth are accessible; you need to know the practical how.

I do try my best to acknowledge the source of all the ideas and principles that I write about in this book; however, through the mists of time, if I forget the source or outstanding principal or world-class insight, then I am sorry to these people dead or alive. If you write to me, then I can acknowledge you in the next edition.

I have listed around 50 books that I have read, and they have all contributed to the person I am now and the success I have experienced. To all of you, I thank you.

Please really enjoy reading this book by implementing its principles, ideas, and pockets of wisdom and enhancing your business, your life, and the life of those people whom you help within your business.

3. Introduction

Do you want to grow a massively successful business and build considerable wealth so that you can be financially free?

How many of these issues and challenges resonate with you in your business today?

- Low, zero, or even negative growth?

- Fluctuating and unpredictable sales, bookings, and cash flow?

- A degree of chaos within your business and personal life?

- A lack of clarity of direction and no exit plan?

- A lack of accountability to ensure that you keep your focus?

- Low or declining profits without a plan to bring about meaningful change?

- A 50+ hour work week and taking home less money than some of the staff?

- Very little personal wealth and certainly not enough to sustain a good life?

- Undertaking too many jobs and even hating the one you used to love?

- A suffering spouse and unnecessary stress back home?

- Are you feeling lonely and isolated with no one to turn to?

Following our Guidance within this book will quickly result in;

- Give you the freedom and time to focus on all aspects of your life, not just business,

- Make you more money than you had believed possible,

- Quickly becoming financially independent with a growing investment portfolio outside your business,

- 20-100%+ sustainable annual growth,

- A systemised business bringing about order and increasing profits,

- Enabling you to build a business that will run without your involvement,

- Being able to spend most of your time with your family,

- Never miss an event with your children,

- A 30-hour workweek or less,

- Working on top of the business, driving it forwards

- Eight weeks plus of holidays per year (no constant calls back to the business),

- Falling back in love with your business

I believe that there is an art and a set of necessary skills that will enable you to maximise your business opportunities, create a real sense of fulfillment, build a massive amount of personal wealth while avoiding messing it all up. I created this book to teach you how to be a winner in business and life.

There is a stark fact for you as a small business owner: 93% of companies registered at Companies House don't exist within ten years. Of the 93%, a tiny percentage sold their business, an equally small percentage were passed on to relatives and then merged the business, and the vast majority failed.

The ones that sold, most of them set out with this intention, and ones that failed didn't set off with any real intentions; they just set off and then fell over?

Keep in mind that there are only two exits from your business; Sale or Fail. Pick one of these choices and make that at the outset, or you are very likely to join the unfortunate 93%

I will state that again, so it sinks in.

There are two exits from your business.....

Sale or Fail.

Pick one now and then aim for that exit.

This level of failed businesses equates to millions of dreams shattered, homes lost and families destroyed every year. The story of misery this brings is immense.

A few of these unfulfilled Ideas could have changed the lives of millions, could have changed o

ur world for the better. What a waste, what a travesty when we have the resources available to reverse the current volume of business failures.

We believe in playing our small part in changing your world and the world around us all for the better, and this was the main reason I decided to write this book.

Of the 7% that survive, many fail to achieve their full potential or start to decline: the remedies to ensure you are thriving and not just surviving in 10 years are all covered in this book.

Of these business owners, the vast majority fail to build up wealth outside their business. When the chance of your business failing is so high, starting to invest from day one is critical to your financial health.

I believe that business founders need experienced and well-meant support, accountability, access to genuine experts, and advice to take them onto the track that will enable them to grow on all levels and to help them avoid the almost inevitable terminal mistakes.

Don't get me wrong here. I want you to make mistakes, lots of them. It's the terminal ones I am keen on you avoiding.

I believe that sustainable growth does not happen by accident and should not be left to chance. No man is an island, and there is no such thing as the 'self-made man.'

I also believe that leaving your growth to chance is likely to lead to your business not achieving its full potential, you have to work even harder than you need to, and you are far more likely to drive your business into the ground.

I aim to help 1 million business founders to have their wildest dreams come true, to build a sustainable business that they love, create a real sense of fulfillment, and build considerable personal wealth that brings about complete financial independence. . .

So let's start your journey…..

4. My Journey

⋅─────⊙⚓☉─────⋅

I was born into an above-average British family where my father was self-employed with two businesses. One he loved doing but made no money and one he hated that kept a roof over our head. There lay a few powerful lessons that I swore not to repeat.

I did not have a drug problem or issues with Alcohol. I was not abused, nor did anything shit happen to me except my dad giving away my dog when I was 16. I'm still pissed off about that.

I'm not one for the 'wow is me' story peddled by many writing business and development books..So that you can 'relate' to my' struggle.' I'm not into b*llsh*ting you.

I am the proud father of two beautiful business investors and entrepreneurs in the making.: Alice (7), Pippa (5). They are already shareholders, and they will probably never have a 'real job' where they work for someone else, building someone else's dream.

Alice is amazingly creative and is building games on Roblox and making money already. I could not be any prouder.

I own two dogs Gizmo and Flossy, 6 cats, and a beautiful house in a beautiful part of a family-friendly little town where the beach is close to hand.

 I Founded The Growth Gurus 5 years ago, intending to inspire and support over 1 million business owners across the globe to grow a successful business, create a real sense of fulfillment and build considerable personal wealth while having fun! And to help them avoid messing it all up, which is surprisingly easy to do.

I have a 25-year history of creating, growing and exciting, fast-paced, disruptive, highly profitable businesses.

I want to add that I also have 25 years of making total f*ck ups that should have been avoided. Not just 'failures'; some of these were very very serious f*ck ups

I started my first business at school with my 'unofficial' tuck shop that outsold the official tuck shop. I had to wait another ten years in the wilderness until I set up my first real business.

I started my first real business at home in 1995, when I founded the first mass-market Personal Injury Claims Business in the UK. Yes, we were the first ambulance chasers, and we laid the foundation of the compensation culture. As a direct result the placed people work, our roads and our pavements are a far safer place.

I recognised that there was a need for a customer-friendly way to make a personal injury claim. We changed the status quo by making a personal injury claim easy, risk-free, and accessible.

I did not create this beneficial model because I was nice, I was only 25 years old, and almost all male 25-year-olds have a pretty selfish mindset. I created this model because it made a shit load of cash with very little work, and it was very easily scalable.

I made a severe error of picking the wrong business partner who spent all the money we made and stifled our growth. So, after two years, we had to start all over again, this time without my first business partner. Major F*ck up 1 cost me at least £200k when that sort of money could buy a five bedroom detached house with an equestrian centre.

My second attempt was way more successful. We hit £1m within three years and within ten years we grew to £15m t/o, 120 staff, helping up to 1000 accident victims per month. In total, we helped 40,000 people source the redress they needed. We also changed many people's lives for the better.

While we were very successful, I did not focus enough on personal development. I also lacked a mentor and a coach for much of the early part of my journey. **Big Mistake that led to major f*ck up number 2**

As a result, while we were massively successful, we messed up far more than we should have done. One of the more significant events resulted in the loss of £7million. Yes, £7 chuffing million. Let that sink in. I made a series of monumental mistakes because I was not accountable to anyone, I no longer had a mentor, my ego started to inflate to such an extent, and I became a total w*nker. Subsequently, my personal development did not keep up with the growth of the business. If you let your business develop faster than you, that typically ends in tears.

This series of mistakes at one point forced my team and me to reduce our turnover from £15m to £250k within a matter of months. One of my business partners even went bankrupt and lost his house. And this was avoidable if we had had the type of support I offer.

Just as this happened, the taxman gave me a personal tax bill of £174k to pay and I didn't have the cash; whoops.

It took me a while to recover and bounce back to create a super successful business. Within weeks I started to realise the extent of my both minor and significant failures that had culminated in me losing a fantastic business and having to work like crazy to build it back up.

This near-collapse was harrowing, where the series of mistakes and errors in judgment that were all avoidable. My experiences, good and bad form one of the major reasons I dedicated my business life to helping other business owners to maximise their opportunities while not falling off a cliff. (I write about your 'why' later in this book)

This near collapse was 100% my fault, and valuable lessons were learnt, all of which are detailed within this book. These practical experiences form part of why I am so passionate about helping over 1 million business owners be the best they can be.

If we had had access to the support we offer at the Growth Gurus, we would have avoided many of our more significant mistakes, had much more fun, and we would have made considerably more profit. Let's not forget that I had not built up any wealth outside the business, so if the business had failed, I would have failed and lost my home.

Don't get me wrong; you are supposed to make mistakes, mistakes, and so-called 'failures' are a good thing. Just don't make the size of failures and errors where you lose £7million, some of your friends go bankrupt and lose their homes. I only survived because I had built at least some assets outside of the business.

Personally, with this type of support offered by my team, I would also have been even happier, made more money, and had much more time for family.

How much did these big mistakes cost me? A conservative estimate would be £15m; ouch. Have I made all this money back yet? I'm working on it!

The advice I would give my younger self? Please read this book, it's all in here!

5. Let's Identify the Issues that are Slowing *Your* Growth

I believe that the first step in growing your enterprise into a thriving business is to identify what is causing your current growth challenges.

Or, if you have yet to start growing in earnest, what will hamper all our efforts to succeed?

I don't mean the symptoms; I mean the root causes. e.g. if you have poor sales, engagements or bookings, that's not a cause for the lack of growth and poor profits; A lack of sales, new clients, or bookings is a symptom of something fundamental that's not currently working.

I believe that simply saying 'we are going to grow by increasing sales or bookings' is a little misguided because it is fruitless to only focus on the symptom. Once you understand the root causes, you can begin working on the solutions.

So, before you spend more money on marketing or attend yet another training course to learn some new techniques, please conduct a brief audit of your business.

Conduct an Audit on your Business

Our Business Audit is a simple tool that graphically shows you where to focus your attention on achieving balance and provides an excellent benchmark to monitor progress.

I cannot remember this Audit's source, and we have used it ourselves and with clients for years.

Knowing where each of your business functions is up to in terms of the key activities is critical to ensure that you maximise your Business's full potential and maximise profits while providing your Business is easy to operate.

Also, understanding what needs to be prioritised first to make the most significant impact will allow you to grow your Business in a managed and controlled way.

A lack of balance in your Business will at best reduce profits, and at worst, could destroy your Business.

By repeating the Business Audit process every six months or less, you will learn how to monitor and track your progress toward your Business growth being optimised.

Results

The immediate result of the Audit is a Radial Chart providing you with a graphical representation of your current position.

The chart will ensure that you are aware of your areas of strength and weaknesses to direct your resources to bring about balance.

Ideally, it would be best to remedy the weaknesses first because this brings about more balance in the Business. For example, there is no point in increasing your sales if you cannot fulfill your client's promises.

The longer-term result is to continually measure your business growth with a simple tool that you can share with your team.

How to use this Audit tool

Complete the questions below and, if necessary, discuss your results with your mentor or coach during your next session.

You can then decide which areas of your business need improvement before taking action.

Leadership

The direction of your life and the business.

Read the statements on the left and circle the number on the right that represents your feeling toward it.

		Strongly Disagree				Strongly Agree
1	I know what I want from life	1	2	3	4	5
2	I understand how the business will help me achieve my goals	1	2	3	4	5
3	I have a 3 year vision for the business	1	2	3	4	5
4	I use my time effectively and profitably	1	2	3	4	5
5	I know my key result activities	1	2	3	4	5
6	What other concerns do you have in the area of Leadership?					
7	Add up all the numbers you have circled and use the list below to determine your overall score. Then enter your score in the box. 0-5 = 1 6-10 = 2 11-16 = 4 17-20 = 6 21-24 = 8 25 = 10					

Planning

Translation into action for all employees.

Read the statements on the left and circle the number on the right that represents your feeling toward it.

			Strongly Disagree				Strongly Agree
1	I have a 3-year plan to achieve the vision incorporating 6 and 12 month milestones.	1	2	3	4	5	
2	Employees understand the 3-year plan and their roles to achieve it including their key result measurements.	1	2	3	4	5	
3	I have an operational plan.	1	2	3	4	5	
4	I have clear score cards for each business objective.	1	2	3	4	5	
5	I have a weekly workshop meeting to track progress on our objectives.	1	2	3	4	5	
6	What other concerns do you have in the area of planning?						
7	Add up all the numbers you have circled and use the list below to determine your overall score. Then enter your score in the box. 0-5 = 1 6-10 = 2 11-16 = 4 17-20 = 6 21-24 = 8 25 = 10						

Strategic Marketing

Strategic decisions that address how you position your product/service to meet customer needs in a competitive environment.

Read the statements on the left and circle the number on the right that represents your feeling toward it.

		Strongly Disagree				Strongly Agree
1	Customers understand the unique difference of our products/service compared to competitions.	1	2	3	4	5
2	We effectively communicate those points of unique differences.	1	2	3	4	5
3	We don't compete on price.	1	2	3	4	5
4	Our products and services have a WOW factor.	1	2	3	4	5
5	Customers and employees find our company story compelling.	1	2	3	4	5
6	What other concerns do you have in the area of strategic planning?					
7	Add up all the numbers you have circled and use the list below to determine your overall score. Then enter your score in the box. 0-5 = 1 6-10 = 2 11-16 = 4 17-20 = 6 21-24 = 8 25 = 10					

Process Systemisation

Actions that fulfil the promise of your Service or Product

Read the statements on the left and circle the number on the right that represents your feeling toward it.

		Strongly Disagree				Strongly Agree
1	We have written, documented, trained systems in all aspects of our business.	1	2	3	4	5
2	The fulfilment/delivery processes are well defined and consistently executed.	1	2	3	4	5
3	"Firefighting" never occurs.	1	2	3	4	5
4	The fulfilment/delivery process is time, money and workforce efficient.	1	2	3	4	5
5	Fulfilment/delivery processes are not a constraint to sales or dispatch.	1	2	3	4	5
6	What other concerns do you have in the area of process systemisation?					
7	Add up all the numbers you have circled and use the list below to determine your overall score. Then enter your score in the box. 0-5 = 1 6-10 = 2 11-16 = 4 17-20 = 6 21-24 = 8 25 = 10					

Winning Teams

Effective overseeing and utilisation of human assets.

Read the statements on the left and circle the number on the right that represents your feeling toward it.

		Strongly Disagree				Strongly Agree
1	The business can operate without me almost indefinitely.	1	2	3	4	5
2	A documented organisation chat exists high-lighting all positions.	1	2	3	4	5
3	Written job descriptions and expectations exist for each role.	1	2	3	4	5
4	Employees "do their jobs" with minimal problems.	1	2	3	4	5
5	The business is not overly dependent on one or a few employees.	1	2	3	4	5
6	What other concerns do you have in the area of winning teams?					
7	Add up all the numbers you have circled and use the list below to determine your overall score. Then enter your score in the box. 0-5 = 1 6-10 = 2 11-16 = 4 17-20 = 6 21-24 = 8 25 = 10					

Finance

Effective Management of Money

Read the statements on the left and circle the number on the right that represents your feeling toward it.

		Strongly Disagree				Strongly Agree
1	The business is never in jeopardy of running out of money.	1	2	3	4	5
2	Bills are paid on time.	1	2	3	4	5
3	Customers invoices are sent on time and to agreement or contract.	1	2	3	4	5
4	Cash flow and profit and loss reports are generated monthly.	1	2	3	4	5
5	The business operates against a budget.	1	2	3	4	5
6	What other concerns do you have in the area of finance?					
7	Add up all the numbers you have circled and use the list below to determine your overall score. Then enter your score in the box. 0-5 = 1 6-10 = 2 11-16 = 4 17-20 = 6 21-24 = 8 25 = 10					

Marketing Communication

How prospective, qualified customers become aware and interested in your products/services.

Read the statements on the left and circle the number on the right that represents your feeling toward it.

		Strongly Disagree				Strongly Agree
1	We have more qualified leads than needed to achieve growth goals.	1	2	3	4	5
2	We have a defined, repeatable process that successfully generates qualified leads.	1	2	3	4	5
3	We can measure the specific impact of each lead generation activity.	1	2	3	4	5
4	We understand the cost of all lead generation activities.	1	2	3	4	5
5	We have a specific, documented system strategy for customer retention.	1	2	3	4	5
6	What other concerns do you have in the area of market communication?					
7	Add up all the numbers you have circled and use the list below to determine your overall score. Then enter your score in the box. 0-5 = 1 6-10 = 2 11-16 = 4 17-20 = 6 21-24 = 8 25 = 10					

Sales

The process by which qualified leads are converted to customers, (new business).

Read the statements on the left and circle the number on the right that represents your feeling toward it.

		Strongly Disagree				Strongly Agree
1	We convert a high proportion of qualified leads and we are constantly improving this number	1	2	3	4	5
2	We have a defined, documented, repeatable process that converts qualified leads.	1	2	3	4	5
3	The business is not dependent upon one or a few sales people.	1	2	3	4	5
4	We have a documented sales process and pipeline that is monitored every week.	1	2	3	4	5
5	We have a documented sales process for add-on products and services.	1	2	3	4	5
6	What other concerns do you have in the area of sales?					
7	Add up all the numbers you have circled and use the list below to determine your overall score. Then enter your score in the box. 0-5 = 1 6-10 = 2 11-16 = 4 17-20 = 6 21-24 = 8 25 = 10					

Graphs

Now transpose your scores from each of the boxes on the previous pages by marking a point on each of the relevant lines on the radial chart below (zero at the centre and ten at the outer edge).

Complete your graph by joining the marks with straight lines as in the examples at the bottom of the page.

Typical Score; Either improve or failure is imminent　　　**Your business is booming Score**

Your Results

Don't worry that your graph looks like the map of the UK. Now that you know where your weaknesses are, you can work on these to increase balance.

A well-balanced business works just like a well-tuned engine and only a balanced business can grow and scale and then enable an exit at maximum value.

Does your result make you feel uncomfortable?

Regardless of the actual shape of your result, it's likely that the current state of your business is down to something even more important, even more, fundamental than this audit can highlight.

If your business is not progressing rapidly, it's more likely that the ***root cause is ....***

You.

The issue is;

NOT the product

NOT the service,

NOT the economy,

NOT your employees

NOT a lack of systems

NOT your clients (it could in part be your clients)

NOT because it is Tuesday or

any other b*llshit you tell yourself.

The primary problem is You.

You are slowing down your business growth, and you are stopping your business from reaching its full potential; **it is you who is the cause of your poorly performing business.**

If you don't like me telling you this, then boohoo to you; get a job.

My book spends much of its content on developing **you first before we can help you to create an audit where you achieve a circle with a score of over 80%**....

It is a *fact* that the skillset and the Mindset of you and your team are **the critical factors** in the short and long-term success of your business and are far more essential than the product or service you offer.

I will repeat that, so it sinks in.

It is a *fact* that the skillset and the Mindset of you and your team are **the critical factors** in the short and long-term success of your business

Your mindsets are far more critical than the product or service you offer, the economy, Brexit, your age, or any other b*llshit story you keep repeating to yourself.

With a Growth, Investor, and abundance Mindset, the ideal skill set, being held accountable, and your dream team supporting you, you can shape your reality, the reality of millions, and change the world for the better.

Regardless of how unique your product or service is, you will consistently fail more often than you succeed in your business and your life until you create a Growth Mindset, learn how to be a true entrepreneur, an investor, and a better person.

Notice that I did not mention 'learn how to do the job the business does' more effectively? That's because it's more vital for you to become the leader and ultimately an investor and not the worker bee or even operator of your business. Focusing on leadership and being the investor is the opposite of what most small business owners currently believe.

We focus a great deal of this book on ensuring that you build the skills you need, create your ideal Mindset, and learn the ingredients necessary to make your business and life far easier and much more fulfilled.

Keep this in mind; growing a successful business is easy; it's you who makes it complicated.

The book also covers all the building blocks you will need to grow a sustainable business. These are not simply theoretical ideas; each section covers the practical steps for you to put the jigsaw of your business together.

6. Are you Ready to Grow your Enterprise into a Real Business?

———⬥——

The vast majority of small businesses are created because an employee (worker bee) was experienced in a particular role or profession, and they wished to work for themselves doing what they did as a job.

They were a worker bee or possibly managing a team when they were employed, and subsequently, they become the worker bee or operators in their 'business'

These people don't create a business, they make a job for themselves, but this time they have a lunatic as a boss. I'm paraphrasing here, and I cannot remember who said that!

There are also many people who attend events promoting a new 'business opportunity.' Then they spend vast amounts of money going on 'training' and 'boot camps regardless of whether they have even a glimmer of a chance of succeeding.. In the UK, examples of this vary widely and include Serviced Accommodation, HMO, BRRR, Property Sourcing, AST, Forex trading, share trading, Amazon selling, Affiliate marketing, business buying, etc

The vast majority of these people then go on to **do** the actual work they did when they were employed, or they have just been trained to do, without realising that they also need to spend time on sales, marketing, IT, recruiting, training, marketing, delivery, accounts, HR, Recruiting etc. as well

They go from being a worker bee to becoming a worker bee with a crazy person as a boss, earning less money and skyrocketing anxiety and stress levels. All the while damaging their health and wealth.

The trouble with being in the majority? You earn what the majority earn, which is typically less than the job you just left. The majority also totally mess up their business prospects from the get-go.

I have a phrase I use often. If everyone is turning left, I will turn right because when everyone thinks something is a great idea, it's typically too late to be a great idea.

Most small business owners also spend most of their lives working hard' and frankly, 'working hard does not make you financially free and fulfilled. If it did, nurses, coal miners, and school teachers would all be millionaires living the life beyond their wildest dreams.

Most of these businesses fail in the first year, and over 90% have died within 5 years. Sadly, many of these need not have fallen if they had learned how to run a business, thinking like an investor and not a worker bee or operator, and developing themselves.

We are **not** taught the skills to run, operate, or invest in a business at school or college. Most don't even educate themselves while they build their small business. Most of the courses people attend don't either. They teach you to be the operator at best and at worst just a worker bee.

Most are taught the opposite skills and mindset that we need to grow a business. So, it's no surprise that most businesses fail, and that's typically because the founder has was unable to develop themselves to enable them to deliver a sustainable business and a great life.

A tiny proportion of enterprises are franchises, and the franchisees are either (a) investors or (b) looking for a 'job'.

The good news, though, is that the success rate of franchises is very high. Why? Because someone else has already designed the systems, the strategy, and the planning. The franchisee, on most occasions, also has fantastic support similar to the support offered by our Growth Gurus.

That said, most franchisees are still either worker bees or operators and not entrepreneurs or investors.

They have 'bought a job.'

A tiny proportion of businesses are founded by entrepreneurs who have very little knowledge of how to do the job that the business undertakes.

They often started the businesses because they wished to challenge the status quo or discovered a market gap.

These people often already understand the concept of working **on** the business to such an extent that they would find it challenging to work in the business, doing what the business does.

These people are true entrepreneurs, actual investors.

These people **do not** attend courses on how to deliver the product or service. They do not attend courses on how to maximise Facebook or Instagram. They send their team on these courses. They invest heavily in developing their teams' ability to deliver and be the best they can be.

The super successful ones don't even operate the business; they are first and foremost the investor. Hence why I believe that creating an investor mindset is critical to attaining financial freedom.

When Branson started Virgin Airlines did he;

a. Attend a course to learn to fly?

b. Check people in?

c. Learn to cook the meals they would serve on the plane?

d. Build a website himself?

e. Use Facebook to attract customers?

No, of course not, so why are you doing this?

Did Richy Branson attend any course to learn any of these critical operational aspects of running an airline? Of course not. If Rick Branson didn't, why do most people learn to be the worker bee or just the operator?

These businesses tend to;

a. Grow rapidly

b. Attract investors,

c. Are far lower risk,

d. Tend to make the most profit,

e. Enable the founders to have a much better life from the get-go.

And there are several solid reasons for this that we will explore within this book.

I know this because this is where I sat when I created all of my businesses. I thought it was weird when someone told me that they worked in the business day to day doing the grunt work, both the worker bee, manager, and operator—wearing all the 'hats' in the business.

When I founded my personal injury business in 1995, of the 40,000 clients we served over the next ten years, I spoke to the first 20 or 30 to understand what they wanted, what motivated them. Then I had no interest in talking to them again; ever.

My goal was to help the 100,000 people to attain the redress they deserved, and I could not achieve that while also working in the business. It just would not have happened.

Frankly, I had no idea of how we served our client's needs from a practical perspective. I understood the why and then built and mentored the team to grow and deliver our value proposition.

I did **not** attend one single course on how to handle a personal injury claim. My team already had the law degree and the Legal Practice course they paid **£30,000** for. I did not attend any marketing courses; my team already had a degree in that. etc

I then set about building my team, and the team did the work. All the work.

How many courses have you attended that focus on building you, compared to courses that focus on the technical aspects of your business? On how to be the worker bee or at best the operator of the business?

Don't stress about that now because now you know. We only know what we know.

The assumption that wipes out most businesses.

With the 99% of businesses where the founder is **not** an entrepreneur already if the business starts to take off, the business will often fail to grow despite the business owner's skills and experience. The business will often fail to grow, or even worse; it will fail. Why is this?

Many who start 'in business' make a dangerous assumption;

Just because you are excellent at *doing* the work (as a worker bee or operator), does **not** mean that you can ***create a business*** that delivers your product or service to a larger audience without expending your time and energy to a breaking point or failure.

This is a dangerous assumption that has led to the delusion that business is 'hard', the needless failure of millions of businesses and will probably be the primary reason for the failure of your business unless the penny drops.

I believe that most founders need to balance three roles in the very early days;

- ✓ *The worker bee;* delivering the value to your clients. i.e. working in the business on the lower value tasks.

- ✓ *The operator;* Who is planning, organising, and supervising others to ensure the work gets done. Still working in the business but on the higher-value tasks. You are also writing the operational systems with your colleagues. (hopefully)

- ✓ Most critically, it would be best if you learned how to be ***The Investor;*** who is doing the strategic work of building the business itself. That entails creating and refining the Vision, innovating how you do things, and identifying new markets and opportunities. i.e. working on the business.

The main challenge is that most founders only focus on the day-to-day stuff because they are the worker bee within their new business. They neglect the more critical areas of being an operator, a manager, and the leader to their people. More importantly, they fail to learn how to be an entrepreneur! How to be an investor.

For example, If you create a business and handle all the business's operations, sales, and marketing, you will struggle to grow a sustainable business. You will increase the risk of you burning out and the subsequent failure of your enterprise. You are the worker bee and not even the operator yet.

Some people believe that they will grow 'organically'; however, this is simply delusional thinking.

If you focus on the day-to-day activity of the business, you are likely to grow for a while and then reach a 'glass ceiling.' This is because you are focusing on working *in* the business, focusing on handling too many roles, and selling your time for money. Because there are only 24 hours a day, there is only so much you can achieve.

Sure, advances in technology will help you, but your competitors are also using these solutions, so they effectively cancel each other out.

Ideally, it would help if you were focusing on the high-value activities where your skills sit. You should delegate all the low-value activities and all the high-value activities you suck at to other people. Within a successful business, you are selling other people's time for money. Successful people buy time. This is very important, so I will repeat this

- Successful people buy time from other people—their employees' and their affiliate's time.

- Successful people also exclusively focus their efforts on very high-value activities where they are superstars.

- Successful people delegate all low-value activities as well as high-value activities they suck at to others and focus on high-value activities only

- Successful people have a Growth, Abundance, and Investor mindset.

- The most successful people think of themselves as entrepreneurs and investors first and don't take on any worker bee or operational roles.

If you are currently running a business and you are still working as the worker bee and the operator, this may all sound very strange to you, even a little impossible. Let me assure you that it's far more difficult to be the worker bee or the operator than the entrepreneur Investor. This book will show you how to escape this slow and painful process and massively speed up your growth, all the while reducing your risks.

If you are happy with being the worker bee, then that's fine: you are simply operating as a freelancer, as one of the 'self-employed,' and you are neither a small business owner nor an entrepreneur. Some people wish to lead a simple life and take on all the responsibilities themselves. 24hrs a day 365 days a year.

Of course, being self-employed is a highly high-risk strategy compared to building a business by focusing on being the investor and not the worker bee.

You may wish to remain a worker bee permanently, or you may want to to consciously delay creating an actual business because of personal circumstances, and that's fine. Just don't take too long or you will form a habit of being in a high-risk environment and suffer a famine to feast income.

We often meet clients who have been the worker bee or the operator in their own business, hitting a glass ceiling for years, even decades, and they don't understand how to create sustainable growth when this is what they want.

This book will help you if this applies to you.

Example 1

A while back, I often popped into this 'spar' shop just off the beach in Blackpool after walking my dogs on the beach.

Over the first couple of weeks, I came to chat to the owners who always seem to be working, whether I went in at 6 am or 10 pm.

I soon learned that they lived above the shop, and I admired their work ethic; however, they were stressed most of the time and working 60+ hours per week.

After a month, I asked the owner why she didn't just employ a manager to do all the work to focus on buying another shop.

She then told me that she was the manager and did not own the business. I was taken aback for the work they put in was monumental and all for just a wage.

I asked who the owner was, and she stated, 'Oh, he owns 12 shops, and he pops in now and then in his Porsche. She then went on to tell me how she felt 'sorry for him because he didn't have a 'real job'. I tried not to laugh at this because she meant what she said. We only know what we know.

So I asked "so would you like to own 12 of these shops'? No, she replied. I really like working.

Now this lady and her husband were real hard workers, and they were happy, as happy as pigs in sh*t. The funny thing is, they were deluding themselves. They were brainwashed into being happy with mediocrity. They are victims of their upbringing and have been sleepwalking with these same beliefs ever since.

The owners, on the other hand, with his 12 shops and probably 20 by now. Do you think he had a terrible life? No stacking shelves, no working 60 hours a week?

What a bummer for him! This chap is the Entrepreneur, the investor, probably making 20 times what they make and working a fraction of the time and having far less stress.

This man and wife team, though, are true worker bees and operators. Both looked 10 years older than they were and were clearly in a constant state of anxiety.

Which position would you want to be in? The worker bee or the Entrepreneur?

Let me give you another example that led to a disaster that we could not avoid.

We were contacted to raise £80,000 for a prospect with crab wholesale business, turning over £1.7m, with the profit being circa £30k. This is how the conversation went;

Prospect; I wish to borrow £80,000

Me: Why?

Prospect; We ran out of crab last year, and so we have run low on cash. (blatant excuse)

Me; Why did that happen?

Prospect; The boats we bought from didn't land enough crab.

Me; How many boats do you buy from?

Prospect; 6

Me; Why just 6 boats when there are 100's?

Prospect; I don't have the time to find others

Me; Why?

Prospect; I am too busy working [on the shop floor] (as a worker bee)

Me; With the 26 workers? Who is running the business?

Prospect: the bookkeeper, but he's been ill (who is another worker bee)

Me; Is he aware that he is running the business? (I was trying not to laugh at this stage)

Prospect; No

Me; Why do you work on the shop floor instead of bringing in more sales or even running the business?

Prospect; That's what I have done since the day I founded the business 23 years ago

Me; Who is running the business now that the bookkeeper is no longer in the office?

Prospect; My cousin and I in the evening and weekends.

Me;   Who has been advising you?

Prospect;   The bank. They keep lending me money, and they keep advising me to expand.

Me;   Has your bank manager ever mentioned that maybe you should be running the business and not working on the shop floor?

Prospect;   No.

Me;   Ok, different question. How do you price your product?

Prospect;   I know what others are charging. (We conducted some market research and found that the prices were 30% under the market rate)

Me;   So how many new clients do you take on per month, and where do you source these from?

Prospect;   Oh, we have not had a new client in 5 years

We sent one of our people to the factory who reported that the situation was even worse. (yes, even more)

Sadly the situation was terminal because the business was saddled with too much debt and legacy issues, and the business failed within a few weeks with the loss of 26 jobs. The owner lost his home, his business premises, and his wife.

This failed business was all his fault; 100%

If we had been asked to assist in helping a year earlier, we would have supported the owner by mentoring and coaching him out of being the worker bee. Or we could even have bought the business off him and let him continue to do what he loved doing; working on the shop floor as a worker bee.

I witnessed the unnecessary collapse of this business, and it was very emotional for all of my colleagues, especially because of his series of misguided decisions caused by a terrible mindset, a complete lack of business knowledge, a lack of accountability, and a lack of professional support.

The moral of this story?

The crab business owner was not working *on* the business, he was working *in* the business as the worker bee, which destroyed his business and his life.

He was as far away from being an investor as he could be.

He was also focusing 100% of his effort on low-value activities at the expense of high-value activities. More on this later

He is currently working as a worker on an assembly line, has no assets, no savings, no investments, and is living in a one-room flat on his own—what a waste.

Can you imagine the amount of regret this guy now feels? Do you think that what this guy did was stupid and you would not do the same?

I have met with hundreds of business owners who have been guilty of the same type of thinking. And before you become too comfortable, I can guarantee that you are guilty of making a number of the same mistakes. If you did my business audit, you would see where you are, the worker bee, and we have a few exercises to test this further.

Critical Tips

Work on your business and not in It. It would be best if you were working on the people who work in your business to succeed.

I will repeat that because this is important;

It would be best if you worked on your people who work in the business to succeed.

Think of yourself as the investor in your business and how you maximise your shareholder value.

Is employing yourself as the worker bee doing all these different jobs maximising your profit from this business?

Would you employ yourself for all the roles you undertake?

Are you now thinking, 'of course not, but how do I afford to take all these people? We answer that question throughout the rest of this book.

I believe that you should work far harder on yourself than you do on your business. Focusing on your personal development will pay massive dividends even in the short term.

Work out the higher-value activities that you are great at and focus all your attention on these activities and delegate all others. (more on this later)

Find a fantastic mentor who has already achieved what you want to achieve.

Working on your business and not in it, or as I prefer to say it; work on your people who work in the business to succeed.

This is where I will tell you that you must start working on your business and not in it to ensure that you grow sustainably, create personal wealth outside of the, work fewer hours, and have fun!

To paraphrase Gerber; you should be working on your people who are working in your business.

Gerber, who wrote The E Myth, introduced this phrase to the world, and it's as accurate now in our internet-based world as it was 30 years ago when he wrote his fabulous book.

What do I mean by working on and in the business?

Working On your business.

If you want to run an uber successful business and still enjoy life you have to know how to play to your strengths and build a team that excels in where you are weak. You may be deluding yourself that it is 'easy to micromanage everything; however, you will not grow your business effectively, and you will find running your business hard work.

You may think that you can get things done better and more efficiently than anyone else, however you can't; this is a delusion suffered by many.

A Delusion!

Thinking only you can do the job best is likely to be partly accurate in some areas of your business, but all the time you are spending doing jobs that other people could be doing even if they are not better than you is time that you are not building your business.

If you do recognise this, then please read on and take notes.

When you get bogged down in 'day-to-day activity that your employees should be working on, you are not an effective leader or thinking like an investor. It would be best if you were also working on the people in your business working in your business.

I'll repeat that

You should also be working on the people in your business who are working in your business.

As the leader of your business, you are responsible for working on your key team to ensure that they are the best they can be.

You may also be sourcing opportunities, spotting issues, and delegating solutions. You are responsible for setting goals, thinking about the future, creating strategy, and planning how you will reach your goals.

How can you do this when you are on your laptop doing the work that the business does? It's impossible to do both effectively and efficiently.

Initially, you are the person in your company who is most motivated to grow your company.. Every minute you spend working in the business by working on tasks that can be delegated is a minute that you are not planning, strategising, and building the best business possible.

Working on the business grows your business; working in your business keeps you stressed and poor.

This is why it is critical to your growth and your wealth to work on your business and not in your business, as the prospect's story with the failed crab business shows.

Because you are in charge of the big picture, when you see areas that need improvement, delegate the work out, so you can continue to be the leader and visionary that you need to be.

It may take a great deal of practice if you're used to getting hands-on in your business, and you may wish to ask your coach or mentor for help with this transition, but your employees will appreciate the trust and responsibility you give them, and you will quickly learn that you can do the job of leading your business that no one else can do

Stop making Pathetic Excuses.

When we ask you to start working **on** your business rather than **in** it, your reply maybe, "How do I create the time to work on the business when I am constantly putting out fires….and I am already working 80 hours a week!!"

That is a pathetic response, and you need to start learning how to replace this mindset and, therefore, these excuses that result in you lying to yourself. Got an issue with this? Then grow a pair and deal with it.

My book will help you overcome your current mindset that creates the delusion that you need to be working in the business to make sure it works.

Also, this book will help you to focus your efforts on building the business and not spending time with low-value tasks that others should undertake.

The more time you spend working **on** your business and **on** the people working in your business, the quicker you will grow the business, and the more time you will find to enjoy life.

This is where using other people's money (OPM) to fund your growth comes in. An increase in your working capital will enable you to work 90% of your time **on** your business and 10% or less **in** the business that will allow you to maximise your growth.

That's because in the early days, while you are more likely to grow much more quickly working **in** the business, you are less likely to have the time to develop the systems that will enable you to gain serious traction. Your cash flow will suffer, and this is why funding your business with other people's money is so vital.

Without using 'Other People's Money', you will need to focus much more time on sales to ensure that your business survives. This means that you may only be able to spend around 10% of your time working on your business, progressing and building it.

Just think about this for a while. Suppose you are spending 90% of your time at the coalface on 'low value' activities. In that case, your competitor is spending 90% of their time working **on** their business, such as developing their people, the strategies, the systems etc(all high-value activities). Who do you believe is going to grow more quickly? Who is going to start taking your customers?

You may forge ahead for the first few months because you are out selling, however soon after, your competitor is likely to storm ahead and rapidly grow, and you will be wondering why you're still operating a small business and still broke after 5 years!

I've experienced this hundreds of times with our clients and once the penny drops, the cash starts rolling in as well as the level of time freedom rapidly increasing.

Are you a Jack of all trades?

Many business founders fall into the trap of doing too many jobs within the business themselves and with most of these tasks being very low-value tasks. In other words, tasks you could pay someone less than £20 per hour to do.

This is a common mistake that will keep these people poor and highly stressed.

Their mistake is to spend valuable time and energy undertaking tasks that they suck at rather than focusing on tasks that they are superstars at.

On the whole, they could also delegate most of these tasks to people who earn less than £20 per hour. They tend to lack focus on prioritising their area of genius, their area of 'flow'

They also neglect to attach value to each of these tasks (more on this later)

Discover your 'Flow' and then focus on that.

Flow is where you find the work easy and effortless. These are tasks that you would undertake even if you were not being paid for it. The opposite of 'flow' tasks are tasks that you suck at.

So, for example, I hate accounting; I deplore it. It's something I suck at so I spend zero hours on it. I delegate every aspect. In fact, in 23 years in business, I have yet to even open an accounting package like Xero. Don't get me wrong, I can read a cash flow forecast, a P and L, and I understand the importance of the numbers. I just don't spend any time producing them, and if I did, I would make a total mess of them.

My Flow? I love talking to new prospects and discovering if they have the 'it' factor in making it in business. I could spend every hour of the day speaking to budding and actual entrepreneurs. We fire each other up.

I love standing in front of a group of ambitious entrepreneurs and teaching them the contents of this book! Not only do I love doing that, I am also amazing at it, or so I am told! I am still working on being humble!

To understand where your flow is within your business and identify the areas you should delegate to others, you can undertake an exercise called the Flow exercise.

This exercise was created by John Wiley & sons.

Would you please list the tasks within your business that you engage in and grade yourself with the following

1. Flow. It's natural, it's easy, and time flies. It is what you are born to do.

2. Excellent. If I undertook this task, I would do an excellent job.

3. OK. If I undertook this task, I would do an OK job.

4. Suck. If I undertook this task, I would mess it up.

Now estimate how much of your time you spend doing these tasks over the month.

Add the % of your time in the quadrants in the figure below.

Without thinking, most business founders, undertake tasks that they are OK or even suck at. They delude themselves that by doing these jobs themselves, they are saving money. They also believe that with practice, they will eventually become better at these tasks. This is a false economy, and you need to stop doing this b*llshit immediately. Focusing on the tasks you are OK or suck at prevents you from spending time doing what you do best.

The last time I watched a football match, I did not see the goalkeeper trying to score goals. If he did, maybe the other side would find scoring goals against his team even easier?

Ideally, you should work out the cost of outsourcing or recruiting staff to handle these tasks and then delegate the tasks to them. Some of these tasks will be of high value and some low value so the cost to you will vary.

You should delegate these to colleagues or to someone outside your business who would if they did the exercise above, would place these tasks within 'Flow' or 'excellent'

Keep in mind that some of these tasks should be classed as very high value, yet you suck at them. Don't be tempted to undertake these just because it's expensive to find someone else to undertake them. By doing so will seriously damage your profits and increase the risk of your business failing.

Personally, I really struggled with this one until my mentor points out that I have been guilty of this. Everyone needs a mentor to remind us of when we are being a dick.

If you don't have the working capital to afford an employee or outsource the task, you should consider bringing on a business partner who revels in these tasks. This is something I have always done, and this will allow your business to snowball.

The Flow Matrix

Use a single sheet and fill in each corner under the headings

Flow   **Excellent**

Ok   **Suck at**

The Get Shit Done Matrix

Over the years, I have devised my version of the Flow Matrix, and you may wish to use this method as well or as an alternative.

The Get Shit Done Matrix

Here is what you do.

Create a list of every task you do throughout the week and weekend. This will take a few days to do. Include everything. If you are married, both of you should do this but do it separately. If you have business partners, do one of these and don't show each other until the job is done.

Make sure you include the jobs you should be doing even if you spend no time on them.

Example;

Task Amount of time a week

Task	Amount of time a week
Emptying the dishwasher	75 minutes
Checking facebook and not adding any value	420 minutes
Erasing my junk emails	140 minutes
Checking my emails	200 minutes
Talking to prospects	600 minutes
Reading a really important business book like this one	300 minutes
Phoning up prospects	300 minutes
Filling in the clients details on my CRM	420 minutes
Putting my receipts in order	60 minutes

Organising my daughters socks	100 minutes
Ironing your clothes	100 minutes
Holding one to one coaching meetings with your key team	300 minutes
Watching netflix	600 minutes
Driving myself to meetings	300 minutes
Commuting	100 minutes
Being driven to meetings and doing High val tasks on the way	500 minutes
Reading to my children	350 minutes
Taking my children to the park	300 minutes
Talking to possible strategic partners	400 minutes
Walking the dog	600 minutes

tip; the last three are all 'high value' activities, and the first three are low value activities even though you may love doing them.

The list should be at least two pages long, and when you add up the minutes, it should take up at least 60% of your time awake. Allow 40% for sitting there like a zombie. If you don't tend to sit around doing nothing at all, you need to go back and think about whether you have missed out on tasks you undertake, or you have your times wrong.

Then write next to each one, the number of minutes per day you spend on each one. If you only do specific tasks every few days, imagine that you spread that time over the week. I have given you an example above. Please don't lie!

Now draw out a big cross, dividing the paper into four equal quarters. Then one by one add each of these into one of the four boxes

High value (brilliant at it)   **High Value** (shit at it/ hate it)

Low Value (shit at it/ hate it)   **Low value** (brilliant at)

Put your answers and the time under the relevant box.

If you are new to business and you are not making much money yet, 'low value' may mean that virtually anyone can do it so that you could pay someone £20 per hour or less.

Once you are growing, 'low value' may mean tasks that anyone being paid less than £50 per hour can do.

When you are Richard Branson's neighbour, ' low value' is any task where some £1000 per hour or less can do really well.

High value is where you would need to pay someone over the amounts you can 'afford.'

Keep in mind that your' hourly rate' should grow as you deliver more to the world, so if you are new, the value you add to the world would be limited, so start at, let's say, £50 per hour and then work slowly towards £500 per hour and above.

Then add up all the 'low value' tasks, and this is how much time you are wasting doing crap someone on £10 per hour could do. Or if you are Richard Branson filling this in, all the tasks that you currently do you could delegate to someone else who earns less than £10,000 per hour.

Personally, I won't do anything less than £500 per hour in value, and I target £1,000 for most of my daily average. £1,000 per hour on a 40-hour workweek is £150,000 per month in income to your family.

When you have completed this exercise, you will realise why you often feel that you have been busy yet frick all has happened. How often do you feel that your business has not progressed?

We have conducted this test on many new start business founders and established business leaders, and results have been mind-blowing for most.

On the whole, most of the new business founders spent most of their time on 'low value' activities and very few 'high value' tasks. 100% of our very successful clients had very few functions within the low-value boxes, and the high-value (brilliant at) box was packed and took up 90% of their waking day.

If you focus half your time on these low-value items, then expect to earn a similar amount as the person you should have delegated this work to…. penny dropped yet? If you do £10 per hour work, expect to earn £10 per hour.

So that's why Richard Branson doesn't fly his planes at Virgin even though he might like to. His hourly rate is probably circa £10,000 and let's say a pilot is £50 per hour.

He certainly does not participate in baggage handling because he would probably hate it and suck at it. Nor does he want to earn the £15 per hour a baggage handler makes.

Now do this exercise every three months and keep a record of your results. The more you do of the high value, and you love it, you will be doing more of what you like doing, you will be spending more quality time with the children, can go on more holidays and make considerably more profit.

To clarify, spending quality time with the family, fitness, strengthening your mental health, etc are all high-value activities. They need to balance with the high-value activities that make you money.

What you measure, you can change.

Remember, if you spend your week doing the work of someone you can pay £20 per hour, you are likely to earn pretty close to £20 per hour.. If you spend your time on high-value activities that are of course, not all financially focused, you will make £millions, and your family will love you for it.

To Recap

- The way your mind is **currently** trained to think over many years of external and personal experiences affects how you see the world and, ultimately, how you run your enterprise. If you have been an employee for years, your mind will have been conditioned to continue to think like an employee or worker bee in your own business. Your mind can be trained to develop a winning/ growth mindset and you must constantly learn new things to win in business.

- Many founders believe that because they are the worker bee and they work on the technical work of their enterprise, they cannot create a business that succeeds.

- To be successful, you need to be great at being an entrepreneur and think like an investor in your business, not a worker bee.

- You must learn to start working *on* your enterprise from the beginning and nurture this habit until you have no other way of operating.

- Conduct the flow matrix or a 'get shit done' matrix to discover where you should delegate tasks within the business; not doing so will cost you your business

- Your focus within your enterprise will be dependent on your personal goals. You may need to revisit these now that you have learned some new stuff.

- If you wish to gain more time freedom, then systemising your business should be a priority, enabling the business to run without you.

- Ensure that you understand the value of all the tasks within your business and focus all of your effort on high value only.

Fund your business properly with Other People's Money to enable you to spend more time working *on* your business to ensure that you maximise growth

Exercise

Write down what you are going to *do* to prepare yourself to start working *on* your business rather than *in* it.

Complete the Get shit done Matrix or the flow matrix and be honest with yourself. Then start to take action!

7. Fostering a Growth and Abundance Mindset

This section on Mindset is the second longest after Increasing Sales Volumes, and that is for an excellent reason.

I believe that nurturing a Growth and abundance Mindset and continual personal development as a whole are **the** most critical ingredients required to maximise your personal and business growth.

Developing your Mindset must be one of your first investments into yourself and then must be maintained for life.

Developing and maintaining your Mindset is way more important than the product or service you provide.

Lets me write this out again;

Fostering a growth and abundance Mindset is considerably more important than everything else.

Ignore this, and your business and personal life are both going to suffer, period.

To gain an even deeper understanding of Mindset, please read Dr. Carol Dweck's excellent book 'Mindset'. This book is on my must-read list for all of our clients. Much of this section uses the principles explained by Dr Dweck, and I hope this section inspires you to devour her book and her many YouTube videos.

Nurturing your Growth and abundance Mindset should be your absolute priority, regardless of whether you are yet to start your business or wish to maximise growth. I implore you to dedicate your time to this subject, or both you and your commercial endeavour will fail to reach your full potential.

Being a business founder is challenging at any point in your development, and, in some ways, that's one of the reasons that makes it exciting. Serious challenges can destabilise even the most experienced of us, shaking us to the point of exhaustion.

Whilst we only have a degree of control of the challenges life throws at us, we can respond with a Mindset that accepts the situation, remaining balanced, and learning from the experience.

This vitally important section explores shifting from a Fixed or Closed Mindset to a Growth Mindset.

You can read much more in Dr Dweck's book.

Going into business with a Fixed Mindset, where you have no intention of changing your Mindset, is very likely to lead to the failure of your business. This is the primary reason why we tend to turn down clients with a Fixed or Closed Mindset who have decided not to develop a Growth Mindset.

We call these 'the Uncoachables'

If you have been an employee for years, you have been trained to have a fixed or even 'selfish' mindset, and you will need to be retrained to be able to be an effective business leader. The same goes for a 'hands on' small business owner where you solely worked *in* your business.

Abundance v Scarcity mindset

One of the greatest mindset shifts you need to be successful in both life and in business is increasing your bias towards an abundance mindset.

Most people tend to have a bias towards a scarcity mindset and the vast majority of successful people have a strong bias towards an abundance mindset.

On a simplistic level, if your bias causes you to view the world as scarce, you will tend to become more fearful of what you can lose. Or you can view the world as abundant and full of opportunity. The stronger your bias towards an abundance mindset will also tend to reduce your anxiety and fear.

Scarcity mindset people tend to:

- Are always fearful of losing things or running out of resources
- Focus on the short-term of every choice
- Evaluate decisions based primarily on risk and loss
- Create anxiety, sadness, and jealousy in their lives
- Believe there's just one pie, and anyone who gets a big piece of that pie is taking it from someone else

I've always found I can't help those with a heavily ingrained scarcity mindset. It's too much work just trying to convince them that they *can* be a successful entrepreneur. We first need to change this mindset, and that's an arduous task.

These people *can* make six figures a year by following their passion. if the market *isn't* too saturated for them to succeed.

Taking a larger slice of the cake does not reduce someone else's pie!

But they don't believe me and probably won't ever believe me. We can thank our outdated, brainwashing school system for much of that. This mindset is only enhanced if their parents also had a scarcity mindset.

Abundance mindset people, however:

- Truly believe the world is full of opportunities for them to explore. Because it is.

- Focus on the long-term as well as the short and medium-term.

- Evaluate decisions with a bias based on gain and development.

- Have a desire to create happiness and success for themselves and the people around them.

- Believe there's no limit to what's possible and what they can achieve.

These are the winners in life and business. These are the people I see do well every day. These are the people who shine when they enter the room. You can feel their energy. They are great people to be around. I surround myself with this type of person.

It's interesting that when we talk to people about funding their business who have a scarcity bias, they tend to focus on the cost of the funding. In contrast, a client with an abundance bias would see the extra profits or the increase in family time. Your scarcity or abundance bias focuses your mind on what your bias forces you to believe.

When we discuss the investment required to take on a mentor, this with the scarcity bias sees the 'cost,' yet the people with an abundance bias see where such an investment will take them.

Many years ago, my cousin, who has a strong scarcity bias, told me about his leaky windows and how cold his lounge was in winter. I asked him why he did not change them? He cited the high cost of a new set of windows, and he didn't even see the value in his family's comfort during the winter or, in fact, that his heating bills would be reduced. To a person with a strong scarcity mindset, they would probably even agree with him!

If you have a bias towards scarcity, this mindset is essential to change and change quickly because what you tell yourself becomes your reality.

Do you want the drafty cold lounge where you need to wear a coat in winter, or do you want you and your family to enjoy the comfort new windows bring?

To change your bias takes practice, lots of practice, and ideally with a coach who can help you realise the bias in your mindset, give you constant reminders and test you as you shift your mindset.

I believe that developing a Growth and abundance Mindset **is by far the most critical personal development you must make to ensure that your business and life succeed.**

Having a Growth and abundance Mindset sees setbacks as opportunities to grow, double our efforts, and even helps us to change direction quickly when we need to.

True Entrepreneurs with a Growth and abundance Mindset bounce back quicker. When setbacks and challenges hit you, a Growth Mindset will enable you to grow while others continue to fail.

A Growth and abundance Mindset will help you see what others see as a failure as simply a learning experience.

Edison once said when asked in an interview if he was disappointed with how often he failed when making the first filament light bulb:

"I have not failed. I've just found 10,000 ways that won't work."

Edison also said:

"Our greatest weakness lies in giving up. The most certain way to succeed is always to try just one more time."

One way to help develop a Growth Mindset is to see each serious challenge as part of a training program to help you grow. Look to learn from each of these experiences. Write it down if that helps.

In time, with a great deal of practice, even the most ardently Fixed Mindset can change how they handle serious challenges that may have seemed insurmountable previously.

Remember that a Fixed Mindset **was created;** it is a construct of your experiences and from your upbringing by your parents and you teachers.

A Fixed Mindset **is not** your natural state however, expect the shift to take work, practice, and time. Idealy use a coach or mentor to work with you to develop your Growth Mindset within one year and not ten. You could even use membership to a Mastermind Group to help you.

As mentioned, If you have been an employee for much of your career, you are more likely to have a deeply entrenched Fixed Mindset. You should not expect to benefit from a Growth Mindset *yet*. You will need to unlearn all the conditioning that comes with being an employee. This conditioning is likely to have started at school and your upbringing by your parents. So there are decades of conditioning that need to be reprogrammed.

Even employed senior management often have a severe case of Fixed Mindset and need to be retrained to think like a true entrepreneur and investor.

For example, one of our clients was convinced that she is only worth £3,000 per month. With this Mindset, then she is going to constantly sabotage her business so that her business profits fit with this limiting belief. So now we are working on shifting her inner belief that she is a '£3000 per month person' to an 'I am a £30,000 per month person.'

I genuinely believe that as an employee moving into business, or a small lifestyle business owner growing their business, we all need "A check-up from the neck up because we are guilty of stinking thinking" to paraphrase Zig Ziggler.

Fostering a Growth and abundance Mindset is very challenging on your own, and our coaches, one-to-one and group mentors, are a massive help. On your own, the process is likely to take years, equating to years of lack of progress, lack of profits, etc.

I strongly recommend that you read at least one personal development book per month and then reread the best of these at least three times over the next year. That's after reading Dr Carol Dweck's masterpiece; 'Mindset'

I also suggest listening to as many audiobooks and YouTube videos on personal and business growth as often as you can. I have compiled a reading list at the end of this guide. See section 21

To shift your Mindset quickly and without expensive trial and error, we recommend engaging a business Coach. The Coach must be experienced in working with clients on Mindset shifts.

Don't just choose your Coach based on how low his fees are: Making judgments based on price and not value is a trait of someone with a Fixed Mindset. Make sure they know what they are doing and an ex-banker will not do!

Quality of service and the value derived is far more important than the cost.

Freelancers, Business owners, and Entrepreneurs all need a coach just as sportspeople do. The vast majority of successful entrepreneurs have used coaches from the beginning of their business careers. This way, they can retain and enhance their Growth Mindset.

✓ Developing a Growth Mindset

Your Mindset will either stifle your growth or supercharge it.

The fact is, having a Fixed Mindset rather than a Growth Mindset, as the name implies, increases the limitations you have in your life and in your business.

Optimists believe the glass is half full, whilst pessimists believe it's half empty. While these guys are debating this, the Growth Mindset guy just-drinks what's in the glass.

The same can be said for those with a Fixed Mindset or a Growth Mindset.

As mentioned at the beginning of this chapter, one of the leading experts in Mindset is DR Carol Dweck, a Stanford University psychologist. Dweck tells us that those with a Fixed Mindset firmly believe that intellect is static, whilst those with a Growth Mindset strongly affirm that intelligence evolves.

In Dweck's book, we highly recommend: 'Mindset - Changing the way you think to fulfill your potential. She explains the differences between the lives of those with a Fixed Mindset and a Growth Mindset. I am only plugging this book repeatedly because reading it is Mission Critical.

Our Mindset stems from our own set of powerful beliefs that we have built up from childhood, our school teachers, our adult life, and our careers to date. Thankfully, beliefs can be changed when they no longer serve us or achieve our goals.

After decades of research on the Mindset, Dweck explains that:

'The view you adopt for yourself profoundly affects the way you lead your life'.

I believe that succeeding in business demands that we engage in the process of our personal growth: **every day**. Developing a Growth Mindset should sit at the core of this personal growth.

This growth process is vital in enabling you to change from a Fixed Mindset to a Growth Mindset.

If you create your business with a Fixed Mindset, you will find it impossible to remain open to being wrong and changing direction, especially if you have been working for someone else for years and you are new to business growth.

When moving from employment or freelancing into running a growth business, it is natural to become overly attached to what we think works and to what is familiar, in other words having a Fixed Mindset.

It is, therefore, vital that you shift your Mindset as rapidly as feasibly possible.

To develop a Growth Mindset, we must train ourselves not to focus on the deficiencies in our ability but rather as a deficiency in our learning or experience. Since we are all capable of learning and experiencing, a systematic learning process needs to be a priority.

A sure-fire way to stop succeeding is to choose to close our minds to change, to learning, and to further develop the depth of our knowledge and insight.

10 Ways to Create and then Improve Your *Growth Mindset*

1.   Every day is a school day!

I believe that you must *not* look for others to approve; you must look to others to help you improve.

"I did not let my schooling interfere with my education," Grant Allan.

If you expend energy to avoid facing obstacles, you cannot maximise upon your current gifts and talents or develop new skills.

Challenge provides you with an opportunity to learn and grow, and I believe that we should actively seek out challenges to improve and grow. The more you know, the more knowledge you develop, the more skills you acquire, and the more value you offer to your clients, employees, friends, and family.

Your willingness to expand and grow places you in an upward spiral of increasing your business's profits, developing and growing your wealth and emotional well-being. Continuous learning enables you to come up with new and improved ideas, which every business needs. New ideas are one of the primary ways to add value to your business and increase your success.

We have included a reading list for you within this book, and you may also wish to listen to YouTube videos on growth. Once you start exploring YouTube, there is enough to ensure that all your car journeys are learning experiences. See section 21

We also recommend engaging a well-trained and qualified coach who will help you to learn more, more quickly, and will help drive your journey to a *Growth Mindset.*

2. Become a curious learner.

Act as a child does daily, live in wonderment, and discover the beauty of life. Decide today to focus on learning and growing continually; I believe that it's one of your primary duties as a business founder, as an entrepreneur.

Begin by asking more questions and being curious about everyone you meet. Ask about the journey they have been on, and what they can teach you.

"For everyone I have met, every experience I have had, teaches me about the world, myself, and others. It is one of the many delights within our lives. The unquenchable thirst for knowledge helps me to move forward with undeniable gusto and provides the deepest sense of appreciation for those whom I have met." David Hargreaves or a more basic version could be

"What I know now is nothing compared to what I will know tomorrow."

3. Develop the Habit of Perseverance

Your frustrations can single-handedly drive you to quit long before you should. While we applaud pivoting, please don't pivot your model just because you lack perseverance.

You must train yourself not to focus on what happens to you but to focus on what is happening for you.

You must discipline yourself to look at what your challenges add to you and your business, rather than on what they take away. We are built to accommodate and to adapt; there is no obstacle too significant for us to overcome.

There is always a way out or another route to get to where you need to go. Marcus Aurelius. This will help you not view setbacks as permanent situations that impede your progress yet stepping stones taking you to where you need to go.

When you believe that setbacks are temporary, you can strengthen and empower yourself and your team.

When you feel your perseverance waning, remember your 'why'. Make sure you have your purpose printed out next to your bathroom mirror.

A great business coach should enhance your perseverance, especially on the days where you feel your resolve weakening.

4. Embrace Challenge.

Growing a business means that challenges are going to appear daily. Challenge is an integral part of all fast-growth businesses.

You must learn to embrace challenges and to see challenges as your friend.

During our more challenging and emotionally strained times, we develop the depth of our character and support the growth of our mindset. Meeting our challenges head-on builds our resiliency to face even more significant challenges to come in our future.

You will also gain a natural high from the endorphins kicking in every time you face a challenge and succeed.

Confronting your challenges reduces your ego and brings the humility of reminding you that there are things that you still need to learn.

"Every Day is a Learning Day" and " What I know today is nothing compared to what I will know tomorrow" are two mantras I have used for the last 30 years!

When you take action in the face of a challenge, you develop a sense of personal responsibility instead of looking to others as a source of blame. This is part of the growth process from an 'employee' or 'closed' mindset to a growth and business mindset.

The confidence and pride of accomplishing complex tasks free up your mind and spirit to be kind, thoughtful, and generous to others, letting compassion rule.

Create your first challenge of the day? How about making your bed? Getting your children dressed? Bringing a coffee to your partner?

Once you have broken the seal of facing and defeating your first challenge, the rest should be easy.

Maybe, one of your challenges could be to create a daily video discussing the challenges that you have faced during your day. You could publish these within the Facebook groups you are in. Only post if your video could help someone. Just don't post crap like most idiots on FB.

5. Embrace Failure.

We should not avoid Failure and then view this as a positive attribute because it is not.

Being 'risk averse' is the mindset of someone setting themselves up to stand still, not to progress. This thinking forms part of the 'employee' or 'closed' mindset.

Failure is just a matter of perspective.

We believe that Failure is just Success in disguise and that in every Failure lies the seeds of further Success. If it helps, stick these phrases to your car's dashboard or near your mirror in your bathroom. I still do this, and I have been in business for over 23 years.

I believe that It is impossible to go through life without experiencing a series of so-called 'failures'.

For this reason, there is no benefit in trying to live a 'risk averse, cautious or paranoid life because your life and business will fail to amount to anything meaningful. You will also build in a great deal of regret, and living with regret should be avoided.

When we interview a client to ascertain if we wish to take them on, I always want to hear about what they call their failures.

Frankly, if I meet a client who has not been brought to their knees at least once or twice, they are either lying or have yet to have grown enough to be one of our clients.

Our more successful clients often come to me with their third or even fourth business, with the previous two or three helping them prepare for this new venture.

Many 'overnight' successes took at least 10 years to be recognised.

93% of the clients we have taken on over the last three years are still operating; a statistical anomaly? No: Business people with a Growth Mindset tend to have what it takes to succeed regardless of the product or service they offer.

It's not the product or service of your business that drives your growth, it's your mindset alongside your skillset.

Doors will open and doors are going to close, and you will make some extremely poor decisions; that's business. It may help consider all the opportunities you will miss if you allow your fears to stop you.

We believe that all founders need to enroll in a group or one-to-one coaching or mentoring program because they will help you avoid making the mistakes that will kill your business unnecessarily. A coach will ensure that 'failure' is balanced with 'success'.

"The only thing we have to fear is fear itself". Roosevelt

"Failure is an effective teacher and success a lousy one". I have paraphrased Bill Gates here!

So-called failures teach us things about ourselves we could not have learned otherwise. Often, our most usable, practical, and valuable insights come only after a loss. Accepting and learning from those insights will be key to your Success. Failure doesn't sound like Failure, now does it?

So does this mean that Failure is simply Success in another form, in disguise even? I believe so, and that's because there are no absolutes in life. Life is not black or white unless you are referring to life or death.

Secondly, there is an old phrase: "good or bad, hard to say". In a nutshell, some of your worst failures are your greatest successes and vice versa. You may not recognise this at the time, and you can only really see these in the fullness of time. There's a great Ted talk on this subject.

Just look back over your life so far. Think about some of the 'failures' that have happened, and then think about what this Failure helped you to achieve. You will see that some of your joyous moments would not have occurred without Failure leading the way.

This quote says it all perfectly, <u>Jackie Joyner-Kersee</u>, a track and field athlete and Olympic gold medallist, explains:

'I derive just as much happiness from the process as from the results. I don't mind losing as long as I see improvement...If I lose, I just go back to the track and work some more.'

It's just a pity that our schools teach children to fear Failure. Schools stigmatise Failure as being bad and to be avoided at all costs. This sets up our children to fear taking action; it teaches our children to be drones.

There is no success; there is no innovation without a whole heap of failures along the way. That's one of the many reasons why my children are home schooled.

6. Ask for feedback.

We believe that the more open you are to receiving feedback, the more you will increase your chances of genuinely serving your clients and, as a result maximising your profits.

Effective and timely feedback will be a critical component of your success and should be used in conjunction with setting goals.

Effective feedback illuminates your progress or your lack of progress.

This type of feedback will help you to determine where you need to improve and the areas where you are doing great. There is nothing more helpful than understanding what is working for you and what isn't.

The primary purpose of receiving feedback is to help you to improve your performance. What's there not to like?

"Your most unhappy customers are your greatest source of learning".

- Bill Gates

When we refuse to receive feedback, we are stubbornly communicating that we are not open or willing to change, be wrong or grow. Such a refusal is a sure sign of a fixed or Closed Mindset.

You should not put off opening yourselves up to honest feedback. By putting off feedback is likely to stifle the growth you desire.

We believe that you should seek feedback from all your leads and clients, even if they did not buy from you. You will learn so much from the feedback that your model will evolve slowly the more you understand your customers' needs.

Receiving feedback that points out flaws in your service should not be ones to shy away from. Feedback gives us a fantastic opportunity to learn and improve your service.

A word of warning. Not all feedback needs to be actioned. One of our clients in the Serviced Accommodation market asked a client about their stay. The reply was overall excellent save for the guest stating that 'I was disappointed that there was no orange squeezer. I hope that our client did not buy an orange squeezer because not all customer feedback has value.

We lost a client recently who had a new start business. The client still had an employee mindset, and we made the mistake of moving her too quickly. Her model was seriously flawed, and we remodeled it together. She loved the result and even said, "wow, you know me more than I know myself; this is the model I was looking for.

The new model required money, and she didn't have any, so we put her forwards for a Start-Up Loan. Because her mindset was still fixed, she could only see that a loan was an expense to pay back; she could not see that the funds would benefit her business. The latter view can only really happen when you have grown your mindset. So she backed off, and her business subsequently failed.

Our feedback resulted in a change to our process. Don't be tempted to move a client along more quickly than their mindset allows.

Practice seeking feedback every day and never stop. Teach your whole team this principle, encourage this principle to become forged into your culture, make it part of your process.

If you have a CRM process, you can build a feedback process that sends out feedback surveys automatically. Then make sure you read these and share them with your colleagues.

Then hold regular sessions with your team where you actively seek to understand the feedback, and together you can improve your model.

That said, be careful to ensure that your people encourage feedback to learn how to do better, not simply to seek affirmations that they are doing well.

7.   Sky Rocket the Self-Awareness of both you and your team.

Become acutely aware of your many gifts, talents as well as areas where you don't excel.

Fully comprehend your key strengths and weaknesses so you can focus on your strengths and source help from others who excel in the areas you do not.

Please don't make the mistake of believing that you should focus on your weaknesses to enable you to improve them. This is a naive method and is often seen in ineffective companies. Build on your strengths instead and employ someone else to cover your weaknesses. Just make sure that they are brilliant in these areas.

You may wish to ask your coach to conduct a profiling test with you to highlight your strengths and weaknesses. Your coach can conduct the same test with all your actual and proposed teams to ensure that they have the talents your business needs to create the complete team.

Ask others for feedback, such as your mentor, closest friends, family members, directors, and colleagues. They can offer slightly different views and give you an overall perspective on what to focus on and areas for development.

Educating yourself every day by reading quality material will support your shift towards an enhanced level of self-awareness. You can even buy CDs and downloads to listen to audiobooks, and there is plenty of material on YouTube to listen to while you are driving along, walking the dog, or even in the bath.

8. Be Inspired by Others.

Those with a Growth Mindset love to see others grow.

Because of their Growth Mindset, seeing others this way adds more fuel to their blazing fire that is alight within, and this helps and supports them continue their journey.

Watching others succeed liberates your soul as to the possibilities of life. Lifting your self-imposed limiting beliefs.

If you hang around people who earn £50k per month, you will soon earn £50k per month. Keep hanging around those on £3k per month don't be surprised that you continue to earn £3k per month. Being with these people lifts or drops you to their level. The same mechanism kicks in if you are hanging around a bunch of losers so choose those you hang around with carefully.

Those with a Growth Mindset have genuine happiness and excitement for others unwittingly attracts and returns success back to them. Keep in mind that you can never receive what you resent in others.

One of the more significant challenges in developing a Growth and winning Mindset is your willingness and commitment to change your most potent beliefs, to wake up to become a new, better version of yourself.

It is now your time to make that decision today, so you can lead an incredible life tomorrow.

9. Spend Quality Time with Successful People.

To develop a Growth and Winning Mindset, you would be wise to surround yourself with people who already have a Growth and Winning Mindset. This group's way of thinking will be contagious, and you will naturally start to develop your Mindset.

There is an old phrase, *"If you're the smartest person in the room, you are in the wrong room"*.

We believe that you should network and associate with business founders, investors, and entrepreneurs who are already growing and are developing their own Mindset.

If you still hang out with your buddies from your old job and are less than supportive, you may wish to limit your exposure to these influencers during the early stages of your growth. Once you have built your Growth Mindset, feel free to spend more time with your old pals. That said, you may not feel the same level of closeness once you have started to grow.

On occasions, you may choose to distance yourself from people who do not intend to grow and become better people. Often these people have a 'toxic' mindset, and these people should be avoided.

You may find that these people are likely to be jealous of the changes you will undergo as you develop. They are likely to want to drag you back to their way of thinking.

10. Develop a morning ritual

Hal Elrod has written an excellent book called The Miracle Morning, and I thoroughly recommend it to be on your reading list.

Hal took some considerable knocks in his life, including a near-fatal car accident that left him in a coma and terminal cancer. As a result of these, he developed a morning ritual that sets you up to succeed.

Hal has developed a morning routine that includes these practices to be carried out immediately after we have woken.

1. Silence. Hal encourages us to meditate each morning and to calm our mind.
2. To run through our affirmations
3. To visualize our goals
4. To exercise
5. To read self-development books
6. To write about our day ahead.

I have to agree with Hal here; setting yourself up for success in business and in life requires you to create the fantastic habit of a morning ritual.

His techniques will enable you to wake up every morning with more energy, motivation, drive, and focus.

These techniques will help drive the shift you need in your Mindset.

To fit in this truly transformational strategy, you will need to be up at 5am most mornings. Don't worry; this will become natural after a few weeks or so!

To Recap

- A Growth, abundance, and Winning Mindset will allow you to bounce back quicker, even without thinking about it.

- A Growth and abundance Mindset will enable you to view setbacks as opportunities to help you move forward and gain experience.

- A growth and abundance mindset will help you see the value in your choices and will reduce your anxiety and fear.

- With a Growth and abundance Mindset when new doors open up when you are faced with a tough challenge and a Growth and abundance Mindset should help you recognise the opportunity.

- A Growth and abundance Mindset will encourage you to ask yourself what you can I learn from each challenge. (even print this and put it on your wall near your desk)

- A Growth and abundance Mindset enables you to be less emotionally attached to the business to ensure that you do what needs to be done.

- A Growth and abundance Mindset will drive you to want to systemise your business to the business that runs without you is a natural state of mind.

- A Growth and abundance Mindset is best supported by a qualified and experienced coach.

A Growth and abundance Mindset will develop more quickly if you associate with other people with a Growth Mindset: choose your friends wisely.

Exercise

Write down the areas of your mindset that you believe needs work and write down what you are going to do to improve your mindset.

Remember to buy 'Mindset' by Dr Carol Dwek and The Miracle Morning by Hal Elrod

Talk to your coach about your current mindset bias and let him or her help you on the critical journey to change your mindset bias.

8. Improve your Effectiveness

Invest your time in what drives you forwards, not stuff that slows you down or even f*cks you up.

We all have a finite amount of time and energy, and so to ensure success in both life and business, there are several areas that you need to let go of or dramatically reduce.

There are, of course, other areas where you need to enhance the amount of time you spend, and this chapter delves into these two areas deeply.

1. Pick your battles.

Focus your efforts on the battles that make the most difference, and ignore the rest. These less essential battles take your time and energy, and it's far too easy to get embroiled in arguments that drive you or your business forwards.

As Churchill wrote, 'You will never reach your destination if you stop to throw stones at every dog that barks.'

When faced with a battle, think to yourself. Is this serving our mission? Is this of high value? Who should fight this battle if it's necessary? However, I do not have the ideal skill set.

2. Focus on high-value tasks only.

In a growing business, the number of tasks that are required can appear daunting. They are only daunting if you are looking at them as all being yours and also if you are failing to assign a value to them.

Delegate all of the tasks that are low value and where you are not brilliant at them. Not doing so will bog you down and drain your energy.

Add a priority level to each of these tasks on your CRM, so when you open your laptop, you can order your tasks by priority.

Focus all of your energy on high-value activities that drive your business forward, keep you healthy, and are precious family activities. Delegate the rest.

3. Understanding that being busy does not equal being productive

I hear from new clients 'oh I am so busy', yet when I ask them what they have achieved today, they can often be stumped. Try to do less of the stuff that doesn't matter or create lots of value and exchange these with high-value or essential tasks.

Take your time to consider the value of a task and ideally identify the value of the task within your CRM system.

If you find yourself 'not busy' and your business and family life are improving then you are most likely prioritising properly.

Next time you meet someone and they tell you that they are 'sooooo busy' ask them to explain, and in most cases, most of this 'busy' are the stuff of little value or importance that could be delegated easily.

On the other hand, if they tell you 'O I have been busy reading David Hargreaves book,' you can congratulate them on time well spent!

Ideally, you should have already completed the Get Shit Done' Matrix

4. Delegate the small stuff

Don't worry for worries sake. Most things are either outside your sphere of influence or not taking you towards your goals.

Just ignore these. Feel free to be aware of things outside your sphere of influence. I love geopolitics, but I don't let it worry me or take up much time. Within the business, I am not concerned with day-to-day low-value activity.

5. Learn not to be a control freak.

Nothing worries me more about budding entrepreneurs to discover that they like to control everything. In my experience, I have found that only complete losers and dicks are control freaks and want to stay that way. Only losers micromanage.

Retain control of your own emotions, your thoughts, and your ambitions. Inspire your team and clients into driving towards success. Once you have lit to touch paper, let go and have faith in your people and clients.

Control what you want the outcome to be, but don't control how they get there. Yes, create the ideal culture in your business but avoid being a control freak.

Don't Micro-Manage; Don't be a Dick.

6. Gain maximum control by giving it away

Surround yourself with brilliant people (smarter than you) and pass responsibility to them. Sure guide these people and help them be the best they can be, but let them control. Remember that micro-managing people demeans and undermines them. Micromanaging is for losers and Dicks.

7. Remove draining people

We all know people who drain us of time and energy, and we receive no returns. If you cannot help them to develop, then get rid of them. They can then pick on someone else.

This may sound a little ruthless, especially if they have been a 'friend' for years. They could even have helped you out years ago. If they are not growing and you are, you need to enable either them to develop themselves and if this is not of interest, get rid of them.

They may be significant in a different team, just not yours. As Einstein said, 'if you judge a fish by its ability to climb a tree, it will live its whole life believing it is stupid.

So let them excel somewhere else.

8. Micromanagement is for losers.

Have faith in your people to grow, develop and then deliver. Sure, you need to train them, and sure you may need to create systems with them; just don't breath down their necks every hour. Not only will this piss them off, but they will soon stop thinking for themselves.

Teach the man to fish…...

9. Avoid time-draining crap

We could end up doing so many things during the day that drain our time and energy, and one of them is social media. Sure, if your business relies on social media to drive business, someone (not you) should be spending time on it to add value and not simply consume it. . don't waste time mindlessly scrolling, scrolling, scrolling. Yes, I know that's easier said than done, and I find myself falling into that addictive trap. Am I sure there are some hacks out there to help you with mindless scrolling?

Avoiding Social media will save you at least two hours a day, which adds up to 700 hours a year. If your hourly rate is £200, then social media scrolling costs you £140,000 a year. Is checking out what your 'friends' did last night worth £140,000 a year?

Checking your emails first thing and then every three minutes is just plain stupid. Stop this one thing to add 2 hours to your day.

Cleaning your own home can waste 2-4 hours per day for people with small children having the most significant burden. Employ a cleaner/housekeeper or nanny and stop wasting your valuable time on crappy housekeeping.

Ideally, use the 'Get shit done' Matrix I explained in the last chapter

10. Complete tasks more effectively using the Pomodoro Technique

Pomodoro is Italian for tomato, and a Pomodoro is a tomato-shaped kitchen timer. The Pomodoro effect was created by Fracesco Cirillo, who was an expert on time management.

Cirillos' time management technique aims to provide you with maximum focus and clarity while enabling you to complete complex or sophisticated tasks more effectively without causing too much mental fatigue.

Cirlllo developed the technique after finding that he was not working effectively because he was being distracted.

One evening he took a kitchen timer (Pomodoro), set it for 10 minutes and then attempted to work solidly for the 10 minutes without doing anything else. He then rewarded himself with a break. This technique enabled him to increase his work even with the extra breaks that he had built-in.

The Pomodoro technique has two elements

1. You work in short spurts to enable your brain to focus on one task.

2. You take regular short breaks that keep your mind fresh, alert and avoids fatigue.

The technique can be used during your day to enable you to handle large and complex tasks by breaking down the task into bite-size pieces by using a timer. I had always used an egg timer because my partner suggested it, even before we learned about this technique. The technique trains your brain to ruthlessly focus on a task for short periods, boosting efficiency.

I use this technique when I am devising and revising a client's business plan. 20 or 25 minutes intense and then 5 minutes break.

Here is my technique; however, the 20 minute part is what works for me, and you may wish to extend this by another 5 minutes but don't be tempted to 'hack' more time by making the time 30 mins because this can have a negative effect.

1. Choose the high-value task and decide to commit to this for 20-25 mins

2. Make sure your phone is not going to disturb you.

3. Close your office door, so you won't be disturbed.

4. Set the timer to 20 or 25 mins and then work intensely until the time buzzes.

5. Take a 5 mins break and every 4 sessions, take a more extended break of 20 mins.

6. If you are interrupted, once you have dealt with disruption, start the timer again.

11. Set up your ideal environment

What's your day currently look like?

Wake up at 7 when the children come crashing into your room? Is your phone beeping every one minute with notifications? By 9 your calls start coming in that you have not booked into your CRM. You begin receiving emails by the dozen, and you reply to them? The staff just 'pop in' for a chat and seem to spend too long?

Before you realise that frick all has been achieved 10 hours have gone by, and you feel as sick as a dog!

Tell the truth, is this your life?

Even if this is only partly accurate, this is all your fault. You have allowed all of this to happen. You have created a 'busy' environment, and without fail, you will waste your days away.

Don't be a 'busy fool', especially since you understand that you shouldn't be doing most of the crap you have been doing.

Here are my tips

1. Make your working environment as clear of distractions as possible. So if you use a desk, make it as clear and uncluttered

as possible and don't face the window if you have people walking by! (I have two desks)

2. Turn off all of your notifications on your phone. Even new emails

3. Turn off the ringer on your phone or even switch it off unless you have a scheduled call and they are calling you.

4. Turn off all of the notifications on your computer or switch it off if you use a pen and paper.

5. Turn off your landline while you are focusing.

6. Shut your office door and put a do not disturb sign up. If you are in an open-plan office, buy a baseball cap that says 'f*ck off I'm busy' or something like that.

7. Turn on music that calms you, and you recognise. (new music forces your brain to think about it and reduces your IQ, so only use music you know well and don't listen to a podcast because you cannot focus on both)

8. Make sure you have enough light and ideally use natural light if possible.

9. Get up at 4-5 am and use a proportion of this time to guarantee focus because no one is calling at 5 am-9am. That's 4 hours where no one is expecting a response from you. I will often use part of this time to send critical emails, and then because I use ZOHO, I can schedule some of these to go later. Most of the emails I send at 5-7 am, and clients notice. I have often been complimented that I am working on their challenges at 5,30am! Clients love it.

If turning off your phone worries you that you may lose business, either route the calls to your PA or a third-party answering service.

Being 'always available' will often diminish your reputation with your potential and actual clients, so be hard to find. Create a 'rarity' factor about you.

I have pre-programmed messages on my phone, and one of them directs the caller to my call time booking tool with Calendly (www.calendly.com)

12. Not all tasks were born equal

All your tasks should have different levels of value and priority.

If you don't assign a level of importance, you will find yourself getting bogged down in too many low-value activities, which will reduce your profits and slow down your growth.

So here's an example. When you first open up your laptop, do you go straight to your emails and start erasing the junk? That's a low-value activity, so stop doing this and let your PA do this.

When you get up and go down to the kitchen, do you immediately start to deal with the dishwasher and re-load the washing machine? Don't do this; assign this to your housekeeper. If you don't have one of these, then a high-priority task should be to source one. 'Housekeeping' is a massive waste of your valuable time and resources.

Also, just because something is urgent for a client does not mean that it should be urgent for you. Frankly, if they have f*cked up and need something sorting asap, ask yourself the question of whether helping this person serves your purpose and your goals? If it doesn't, kindly ask them to join the line. If you lose this client, then good; they were not an ideal client who valued your time.

I like to assign a level of importance to all the tasks on my CRM from low to high value.

I use my 'Get Shit Done' Matrix.

This tactic enables me to delegate all of the lower-value tasks to colleagues who will rattle these off quickly. On any one day, I can have 70-120 new tasks, and this means that I can delegate the 80% that are low value or are high value, but I suck at them.. My PA's do this because they are far better at placing a value on the tasks than me, and secondly, assigning a value is a low-value activity. Oh the irony.

What value you put on tasks and which ones you deem appropriate will depend on the value you assign to your time.

I set my minimum at £200 per hour at the moment; however, it's typically £500 per hour. (I'm setting up a few new businesses, and there is a lack of people to delegate to, just at this moment). That's in the immediate value, not the future value. Anything less than this is delegated. The trouble is, if you value your time at just £20 per hour because you are new to business and your employer paid you this, you will handle low-value tasks.

When you start assigning value levels or importance to your tasks, you will see how many tasks you can delegate to colleagues or can be handled by your PA.

At first, you will feel a little 'lost' because you don't have that 'busy' feeling. The great news is that you can now focus on all of those high-value tasks and activities that help you become the best you can be and drive your business forward more quickly and effectively.

Some tasks are 'priceless' or have an immense value. So, for example, I am assigned to wake and dress my two daughters, Alice and Pippa. I could delegate this to their Nanny however, this task is 'priceless' and is, therefore, 'high value'. Your daughters are not 5 and 7 forever.

Walking the dogs is also a high-value activity. Firstly it's exercise, which has a high value, but it's also excellent thinking time.

Reading is ultra high-value time, and if the book you are reading is as stunningly valuable as this one, then I assign a value of £5,000 per hour on reading. If £5,000 seems excessive to you, think of the value that has been added to your life because of some of the books you have read. Really think about that.

I recently spoke to a client, and they confirmed that 'Rich Dad Poor Dad had changed their lives. I asked them to assign a lifetime value to the ideas that they gleaned from the book. The answer? £10m. They have read this book 5 times, each being 10 hours, so that's £200,000 an hour. £5,000 doesn't seem so much now does it?

Filling your emails and getting rid of the junk emails should start to feel like a low-value activity now…..

Do not do DIY on anything unless it's high value and you are brilliant at it.

Unless you are brilliant at it, DIY is a recipe for disaster and will likely cost you valuable time and energy. If you are new to business or still subscribe to the false belief that business is about 'hard work', please read this section carefully.

By way of an example, we are all told about Edison and his 10,000 attempts to make the light bulb. Edison did not test 1 of the 10,000; he had a team of experts do the work. But he is the one who had the perseverance to undertake 10,000 failures.

When you are considering your tasks, don't ask yourself the question 'how' questions. ie

1. How can I do this?
2. How can I fit this into my schedule?
3. How can I assign this to someone better, smarter, cheaper, and more efficient than me?

Once you have used my 'Get shit done' Matrix, II suggest that you asked yourself 'who' questions

1. Who is best placed to undertake this task?
2. Who would love to take on this task?
3. Who would find this task much more straightforward than me?
4. Who is an expert in this area?
5. Who is less costly than me?
6. Who is already undertaking similar jobs?

Once you have a PA, this task becomes increasingly easier.

There is no such thing as multitasking.

Task jumping and multitasking are sapping your effectiveness. Your brain can only handle one task at once, and you are deluding yourself if you believe that you can 'multitask'.

Every time you jump from one task to another, your brain takes both time (at least 27 seconds) and energy to switch from one task to another. The average person will task jump 200-300 times a day, and each time the brain needs 27 seconds to refocus on the task you have jumped to. That's a great deal of time with your brain switching from one task to another.

So when you are in the middle of a task, and you are within your '20 minute' focus time, don't be tempted to check your emails, your Facebook feed, your LinkedIn.

Employ a PA; a real live one.

Your first employee should always be a fantastic PA, a real one and not one of these virtual ones.

A PA will handle all of those 'lower-value tasks and even employ her own team to churn through them all effectively and profitably.

Let your PA work with you to develop the systems in your business. A great PA is likely to be considerably better than you at admin and systemising.

Let them keep you focused on high-value activities and let them run your diary.

A great PA is a strong-willed individual and doesn't take s*it off anyone, and this includes you.

If you are still relatively small, less than £1m t/o, then a great PA should double your profits within a couple of months.

Don't scrimp and employ an idiot or a wallflower. Pay for a quality person because you will make 10x their cost.

Lastly, please don't employ one of these so-called 'virtual' PA's unless its for a very specialised service.

Exercise

List all of the things in your life that are draining your time and energy and then dedicate yourself to erase these by giving them to your PA or dropping them completely.

If you have yet to complete the 'get shit done' Matrix then do that now.

Decide how you are going to set up your environment to be ideal for getting sh*t done.

List the jobs you are going to do to create your ideal environment for focused work. Then delegate all the low value ones.

9. Develop your Core Purpose to Sustain you.

To sustain your business over the long term and to ensure that you and your core team are happy and fulfilled, you need to find both your personal purpose *and* the purpose of the business.

Simon Sinek calls it your 'Why' (Although I'm not a fan of Sinek's idea that you should start with the why)

If cash flow is a major headache for you now or you make your targets purely cash-focused, just solving these issues is unlikely to increase your happiness over the medium to long term. True fulfillment comes from when your deepest needs are satisfied: your drive for meaning.

Maslow's Hierarchy of Needs explains the four levels of human needs:

- Survival and safety needs; food, clothing, shelter, security (most basic needs).

- Social needs: participation, belonging, love, friendship, intimacy (slightly higher order of needs).

- Esteem needs: ego gratification, status, place in society (high level needs).

- Self actualisation: the need to realise your potential by having a meaningful impact on the world (highest level of need).

Maslow's model suggests that each of these needs are critical to our happiness. Once each of the levels is met, they stop affecting our happiness levels.

Eg. There is a limit to how much food, clothing, or shelter we need. Of course, you may desire or want more; you will often enjoy the immediate gratification of more. However, this is unlikely to make you any happier and may even make you unhappier. Unless, of course, you are as shallow as a puddle.

In other words, as a business owner, once the lower orders are satisfied, there remains a craving for something deeper, something 'more'.

I believe that this is the primary reason why many people with a 'lifestyle' business often become frustrated, bored and start hating their 'business'.

- Searching for your true meaning, your 'Why'

True happiness starts with engaging in meaningful activity.

When you feel happier, more resilient, and more able to handle stress, you are more likely to have the focus and consistent motivation required to run a successful business and have a happy and fulfilling personal life.

While we may be able to increase our feelings of happiness by, let's say, going on holiday, eating that KFC, or taking a stroll in the sun with your dogs, these activities are focused on you, and therefore don't usually create meaning. (although walking your dogs helps you come up with great ideas and keeps you fit!)

Typically when we focus on others, not ourselves, we derive most meaning and fulfillment and ironically more satisfaction, profit, and wealth.

When you (and your business) focus on the impact you can make on others and the world, you will often find the most meaning, happiness, and more profit.

So, make sure your business culture is focused on the people; your management team as well as your clients.

- Understanding your Personal Purpose.

I believe that if you want a business that inspires, energises, and fulfills you and your whole team to ensure that it makes a real difference to the world, then aligning the business with your purpose is **very** *very* important.

To Recap

- Fulfillment is sustained by living your life and running your business meaningfully.

- When you are happy and fulfilled, you are more able to handle the cut and thrust of business life and have the focus and motivation required to maximise your full potential.

- We experience more meaning when we focus outward on the contribution and value we add to others.

- Use the 'finding your purpose' exercise to help you identify your unique purpose.

- Finding your meaning and then focusing on others (clients and customers) is likely to lead to considerably more profit and personal growth.

Exercise

Please work on this exercise to work out what is truly important to you; your core purpose.

1. Use the space below to write the main points of a 5 minutes introduction speech for your son or daughter to make on your 80th birthday where you will speak about your life so far after their introduction.

2. Scan through what you wrote for the more important words and phrases and highlight them

3. Look for shared ideas and themes within the highlighted parts.

4. Group any common ideas into main themes.

5. Identify the central idea, word, phrase or sentence that integrates each of your themes.

This is not easy to do, and you may wish to involve your business mentor or coach to help you.

You may wish to read Simon Sinek's book on the subject. 'Start with Why'

10. Developing the Core Purpose for your Business

I believe that to build a long-term, sustainable and fulfilling business; you need to start at the beginning: defining the Purpose of the business.

I believe that your personal Purpose should align with the Purpose of the business, or you will not be able to remain engaged and excited about your business, and it will fail to perform.

I once created businesses that did not resonate with my personal Purpose and quickly became disinterested and exited rapidly. If this is your current situation, then you need to act quickly.

I even had one business where my fellow shareholders did not share my core purpose, and I just had to walk away. That was very tough to do because I had so much invested in it, but it had to be done.

Your team's values and Purpose must also align with the Purpose of the business. Hence why later, I write about recruiting for attitude and not aptitude.

Your business needs an outward-focused and meaningful purpose in the same way that our lives do. Put simply, your business should laser focus on delivering valuable benefits to the people it serves, which means the customers, employees, and stakeholders.

While specific financial goals are critical, they must be driven by a more fundamental, underlying business *Purpose.*

To ensure that you sell your products and services to a growing audience of happy customers, you need to deliver value to satisfy your customer's needs. Most of your customers must have a deep connection with your values to buy from you.

So the crystal clear, universally understood Purpose of your business should mean that your team is exclusively focused on the right goal i.e, truly understanding and satisfying your customers.

Suppose your team is laser-focused on satisfying the customers' needs and wants. In that case, you are more likely to build a more significant and more sustainable business that generates more money from happier customers, who are more likely to rave about you on LinkedIn and social media.

The most successful companies go one step further. It's not just about satisfying customers; it's about finding a purpose, something to stand for....something beyond profit. More and more customers prefer, trust and support businesses that stand for something worthwhile and essential.

Adopting this philosophy helps your business stand out in our Peer review world of Google, Facebook, and LinkedIn.

My daughter's last school has a purpose, and that is to 'make the next generation of leaders.

A client of mine who sold fire safety equipment has their Purpose; to protect life and property. To them, saving a life is a meaningful way to make a difference in the world. That's great because selling fire extinguishers would be tremendously dull without this powerful Purpose.

Our Purpose? One of our businesses helps people to invest in high yield investments.

Our Purpose; To help 1 million people achieve financial independence or financial 'freedom' by nurturing an investor mindset and helping them source the investments they need to achieve their goals.

Purposes such as these inspire ongoing motivation for you and all of your people far more than simply focusing on the money or targets. When you, your directors, and staff feel they are doing something important, you will all be much more motivated.

If you want to impact the world positively, if you hope to leave a lasting legacy, if these ideals lie within the centre of your personal core purpose, only a truly inspiring business purpose will drive you and maintain your energy, passion, and commitment.

When that happens, your business and effectiveness will reach the stars.

If your staff feel as though they are all working towards something bigger, something that makes a difference and is super important, they will also be more motivated and far more productive. Your team would be working for the 'purpose' and not for money. Reinforcing your business purpose is likely to have a fantastic effect on your culture and your results.

Define and Refine your Business Purpose

Here is an interesting exercise that you can try yourself or alongside your coach to uncover your core purpose. It's called 'The Five Whys'. Start by describing the product or service your business provides. Then keep asking yourself, "why is that important" until you reach your core purpose.

For example, here is how The Five Whys worked for The Growth Gurus, our Mentoring business.

Q. Describe the service you offer.

A. We help our clients to build a more meaningful, profitable business while growing their wealth and retaining their well-being. We achieve this by supplying all the support, advice, and tools they will need throughout the life of the business. (this is the 'what we do')

Q. Why is that important?

A. Our clients stand a much better chance of maximising their businesses' true potential, maximizing the business's value, maximising the growth in their wealth, reducing their risk of failure, and having fun doing so.

Q Why is that important?

A. Our clients gain the freedom to live genuinely independent lives by helping others to fulfill their wants and needs.

Q. Why is this important?

A. This enables each of our clients to improve the lives of millions of people.

What a purpose! What a legacy! As you can imagine, this is a superb purpose that fires up our team to do the best we can.

We often receive calls asking us to raise money to enable a client's business to grow. Do you believe that having these values ensures that we help our clients achieve more? Damn, right it does.

Our core purpose is to enable our clients to improve the lives of millions of people as well their own and hopefully make the world a much better place…now try the same exercise on yourself or even ask your coach to assist you make the most out of this exercise.

You can use the five whys method to solve many of your business challenges. Your coach should be able to help you with this. I believe that you need a coach or mentor for this exercise because when you are asked by someone else, you give far more accurate answers.

To recap

- Your business must have a meaningful purpose in the same way your life needs one.

- To maximise your potential, you and your team must all focus on fulfilling a valuable purpose for your clients and customers.

- Clients prefer to trust and rally behind businesses that stand for something worthwhile and essential.

- A succinct and clear purpose will inspire you and your team and give you the required motivation to get through the tough times.

- Use 'The Five Whys' test to uncover your business purpose.

Exercise

Define your Business Purpose

Here is an interesting exercise that you can try yourself or alongside your mentor or coach to uncover your core purpose. It's called 'The Five Whys'.

Start by describing the product or service your business provides, as I did above. Then keep asking yourself, "why is that important" until you reach your core purpose.

Ideally, you should use your mentor or coach for this task because I have found that you will lie to yourself and your why will be what you have been conformed to believe in.

If you are a member of one of our Mastermind Groups, you could use one of your group sessions running through this process together.

11. Create Your Personal and Business Goals.

Have you thought about what you want to have personally achieved over the next one, two, or five years?

Are you clear about what your main objectives are within your business over the same period? Are these objectives in harmony with your personal goals?

Often I come across unhappy business founders whose life goals are out of sync with their business goals. This never ends well. Never.

Think about this for a moment. Let's say that you wish to earn just £20k per month after tax and pension contributions, yet you want your business to grow to £5m pa in sales and £1m in profit.

So, in this example, your company is four times as big as it needs to be; why?

Would it not be more ideal to match both your personal and business ambitions?

Do you know what you want to have achieved in your personal life and your business by the end of today, this week, this month, never mind over the next five years?

If you want your business to succeed and reach your personal objective, you need to set goals.

Without goals, you will lack focus and direction, even with an incredible personal and business purpose.

"An idiot with a plan can often achieve far more than a genius without a plan". Warren Buffett, a personal hero of mine

Goal setting not only allows you to take control of your life's direction; they also provide you with a benchmark for determining whether you are succeeding.

Think about it: Having £10m in the bank is only proof of success if one of your goals is to amass riches. If your goal is to practice acts of charity, then keeping the money for yourself is suddenly contrary to how you would define success.

To accomplish your goals, you need to know how to set them so that you can achieve them.

You can't simply say, "I want" and expect it to happen.

Goal setting is a process that starts with careful consideration of what you want to achieve and ends with a lot of hard work actually to do it.

In between, there are some very well-defined steps that transcend the specifics of each goal.

Knowing these steps will allow you to formulate goals that you can accomplish.

Here are our eight golden rules of goal setting.

The Eight Golden Rules

1. Set Goals That Motivate You

When you set goals for yourself, it is essential that they motivate you: this means making sure that they are imperative to you and that there is value in achieving them.

If you have little interest in the outcome or are irrelevant given the larger picture, then the chances of you putting in the work to make them happen are slim. Motivation is a critical key to achieving goals.

Set goals that relate to the high priorities in your life. Without this type of focus, you can end up with far too many goals, leaving you too little time to devote to each one.

Goal achievement requires commitment, so to maximise the likelihood of success, you need to feel a sense of urgency and have an "I must do this" attitude.

When you don't have this, you risk putting off what you need to do to make the goal a reality.

This, in turn, leaves you feeling disappointed and frustrated with yourself, both of which are de-motivating. And you can end up in a very dangerous position by reinforcing or even creating a closed mindset.

You must set your personal goals first, and then you set your business goals to enable you to achieve a number of your personal goals.

Top Tip:

To make sure your goal is motivating, write down why it's valuable and important to you.

Ask yourself, "If I were to share my goal with others, what would I tell them to convince them it was a worthwhile goal?"

You can use this motivating value statement to help you if you start to doubt yourself or lose confidence in your ability to make the goal happen.

We do suggest that you use your coach when setting goals.

Your coach will hopefully be highly trained in establishing an excellent goal structure and will also make you accountable for your progress.

So can being part of a Mastermind Group www.thegrowthgurus. co.uk/mastermind

2. Set SMART Goals

You have probably heard of SMART goals already. However, do you always apply the rule?

The simple fact is that for goals to be powerful, they need to be SMART.

There are many variations of what SMART stands for, but the essence is this –

Goals should be:

- Specific.
- Measurable.
- Attainable.
- Relevant.
- Time Bound.

3. Set Specific Goals.

Your goal must be clear and well-defined.

Vague or generalised goals are unhelpful because they don't provide sufficient direction.

Remember, you need goals to show you the way.

Make it as easy as you can to get where you want to go by defining precisely where you want to end up.

A real example of one of my clients who achieved all of these goals (dates have been altered);

- I will take time off from the business and take my daughters for six months' holidays every year.

- We will buy a holiday home in Portofino, Italy, with a value of $3m by May 2022. This will mean that I will need a deposit of £300,000 and repayments on the mortgage of $10,000 per month. This will require my businesses to make an extra $40,000 per month to pay for this.

- To buy a home on the shores of Lake Windermere with a value of $5m by May 2023. This will mean that I will need a deposit of £1.5m and repayments on the mortgage of $5000 per month. This will require my businesses to make an extra $20,000 per month to pay for this.

- My partner and I will give $1000 per month to various charities by December 2022, increasing this by $1,000 each year.

- We will be paying down the mortgage on our main home at the rate of $5000 per month for the next five years, and this requires our businesses to make an extra profit of $20,000 per month to pay for this that I can drawdown.

- My partner and I both wish to have $2m in each of our QNOP pensions within five years of today. In the first year, starting June 2021 I wish the company to make a pension contribution of $5000 per month into our pension with $20,000 per month during the next year and $30,000 per month in the following year.

- My partner and I both need a new Range Rover in November 2021 and every two years thereafter. This will cost $2,500 each and that equates to $10,000 in extra profits per month.

- My partner and I both wish to have a property portfolio run fully by our team worth $20m by 2025, giving us an income of $700,000 pa.

These goals require an increase in profit to take out of our businesses of **$250,000 per month** to finance these goals. We will also need circa $2m in cash to fund the deposits.

Notice that our client is taking out their profit and then investing this into income-generating assets. Don't be one of those fools who keeps all their profit in their business. More on this later.

4. Set Measurable Goals

Include precise amounts, dates, and so on in your goals so you can measure your degree of success.

If your goal is simply defined as "increase monthly drawings," how will you know when you have been successful?

In three months if you have an increased monthly drawing from $3,000 to $5,000 or in two years when you have increased drawing to $100,000 per month?

Then break this down into daily targets. $3,000 per month is only around $250 per day before tax.

An income of $100,000 per month is still only $5,000 per day in gross revenue. Sounds easier now, doesn't it?

Ps. Do you think that **$5,000 per day** is a lot? Yes? That's because of your limiting beliefs and not reality. There are over 10 million people in our world that take far more than this out of their businesses, and you can be one of these or not; it's your choice.

Without a way to measure your success, you miss out on the celebration that comes with knowing you have achieved one of your interim goals.

Then put a chart on the wall of your office so you can track your daily target. There is also a cool software to help you track your goals http://www.mipurpose.com

5. Set Attainable Goals

Make sure that it's possible to achieve the short-term goals you set. We are not writing about your stretch goals here.

If you set a short-term goal that you have no hope of achieving, you will only demoralise yourself and erode your confidence.

However, resist the urge to set goals that are too easy.

Accomplishing a goal that you didn't have to work hard for can be anticlimactic at best and make you fear setting future goals that carry a risk of non-achievement.

By setting realistic yet challenging goals, you hit the balance you need. These are the types of goals that require you to "raise the bar," and they bring the greatest personal satisfaction.

6. Set Relevant Goals

Goals should be relevant to the direction you want your life and business to take. By keeping goals aligned with this, you'll develop the focus you need to get ahead and do what you want.

Set widely scattered and conflicting goals, and you'll fritter your time – and your life – away.

The example goals I wrote earlier were very family orientated ie education, holidays, second home, paying off the mortgage.

7. Set Time-Bound Goals

Your goals must have a deadline. Again, this means that you know when you can celebrate success. When you are working on a deadline, your sense of urgency increases, and achievement will come quicker.

8. Put Your Goals in Writing

The physical act of writing down a goal makes it real and tangible. You have no excuse for forgetting about it. That's writing with a real pen or stylus and not typing. You can type the goals up later.

As you write, use the word "will" instead of "would like to" or "might."

For example, "I will increase my profit from $100,000 to $500,000 this year," not "I would like to increase my profits."

The first goal statement has power, and you can "see" yourself driving up sales; the second lacks passion and gives you an excuse if you get sidetracked.

9. Frame your Goal Statement Positively

If you want to increase the number of Serviced Accommodation units, you have "I will increase the number of units by at least 1 per week over the year" rather than "I will increase the number of units to enable me to leave my day job."

Or

Suppose you want to increase the number of Limited companies. In that case, your accountancy practice has as clients, "I will increase the number of limited companies engaging us by 10 per week." rather than " "I will increase the number of limited companies engaging us to counter the ones that leave us."

The first one is motivating; the second one still has a get-out clause "allowing" you to succeed even if you are way off what you are capable of achieving.

10. Make your Goals part of your daily routine.

If you use a To-Do List, make yourself a To-Do List template with your goals at the top of it.

If you use an Action Plan, then your goals should be at the top of your Project Catalogue.

We hope you are using CRM and that your 'to do list' is now part of your task list.....

Post your goals in visible places to remind yourself every day of what you intend to do.

Put your goals on your walls, desk, computer monitor, bathroom mirror, car, or refrigerator as a constant reminder.

If you do use CRM, then add your goals into the diary section of the CRM so you can see them daily. Break down each goal so each day you can keep on top of each of these goals

Top Tip:

Make sure you have a mentor or coach and be a member of a Mastermind Group so they can keep track of your goals, and then they question your progress. No matter how important you are, you need someone to answer to!

11. Make an Action Plan

This step is often missed in the process of goal setting.

You become so focused on the outcome that you forget to plan all of the steps that are required along the way.

By writing out the individual steps and then crossing each one off as you complete them, you'll realize that you are making progress towards your ultimate goal.

This is especially important if your goal is big and demanding or long-term. Read the section on Action Plans for more on how to do this.

Ideally, you should use your coach to help you with this step.

12. Stick With It!

Remember, goal setting is an ongoing activity, not just a means to an end.

Build-in reminders to keep yourself on track, and make regular time-slots available to review your goals.

Your end destination may remain quite similar over the long term, but the action plan you set for yourself along the way can change significantly.

Make sure the relevance, value, and necessity remain high.

13. Being accountable to others

Being accountable for others is a huge help. Ideally, join a Mastermind Group, and your Mentor can support you. Many of our clients use both, and because they have these weekly meetings, they are very conscious that they will be reporting to their Mentor and their peers in the Mastermind Group.

Can you imagine telling your peers in your Mastermind Group about your goals and what you need to do to achieve them? Are you going to slack off and forget about what you have said you will do and then announce this to your peers, to your coach?

Hell no, you will make sure that you stick to these goals!

To Recap

Goal setting is much more than simply saying you want something to happen.

Unless you clearly define exactly what you want and understand why you want it in the first place, your odds of success are considerably reduced.

By following my eight Golden Rules of Goal Setting, you can set goals with confidence and enjoy the satisfaction that comes along with knowing you achieved what you set out to do.

You may decide that you should consult with your coach, and you must include your closest family.

Exercise

Write down your top 3 goals and follow the principles in this chapter.

Then test these with your Mastermind group colleagues along with your Mentor and or coach.

12. The Business Journey

As entrepreneurs, we all have our great business ideas, and then we start to build our business to deliver the service or product.

We set up the business, build a website, open a bank account, and then we are off! . Soon after, most of us fail, and there are reasons why.

It's helpful to think of your business as a car, a car we need to take us on our journey, and a final destination where we would like to be in 1, 2, 3, and 5 years. Reaching your final goal and the waypoints on the way are primarily down to the car's performance you are driving to get there.

Those in business without a car are called the self-employed.

The car in the diagram below represents the typical business journey of someone who makes it by building, scaling, and then selling the business. By using this diagram, you will soon see where you are on this journey.

THE BUSINESS JOURNEY

Your New Business
You are Pushing it

You are full of
energy and off you go!!

Your business has
no engine and pushing
is hard work.

You Still
Pushing !

Idea !
Build an Engine!

You Build the
engine

Your engine improves
and you grow!

Sell and make £millions

8 Millions

STARTUP	STRUGGLE	BUILD	SCALE	SELL
You are really excited and this gives you the energy to create early momentum.	You will soon become tired pushing your business. Far something .... Most Business fail here.	You then start to build the business engine and you start to grow!	You keep imroving the engine and you grow rapidly.	You will now start earning real money by selling your business. Enjoy your financial freedom

At the beginning of the business journey in the diagram, the business is very new. It typically has low levels of resources, zero processes, and zero systems required to grow. The great news is that as the founder, we tend to have bucket loads of energy and enthusiasm at this stage and all they need to do is give it a push, and off they go. (hence the downslope in the diagram)

At this stage, most newbies in business have zero experience of driving the car.

After a short time, the car starts to slow down, and this is where the newbie begins to push the car (the business); however, pushing your car is hard work and far from ideal.

The newbie is pushing it because the car has no engine.

I'm sure when you bought your car, you wanted to get in and drive and not just push it along the road, but that is exactly what 98% of newbie entrepreneurs do. It's not a bad thing as long as you take action to build your business engine.

At this stage, you have the business ie the car, but you don't have the engine, and you have no petrol/ diesel/ gas (cash). The only resource you have is your energy to push the car. This stage is where 90% of businesses stay, often for years and, on occasions, decades. Until the business inevitably fails or you realise that there is another way to get to where you would like to go. If you are at this stage, you either need to take action, or life will be tough, very very tough.

It's at this stage of realisation when most of our clients get in touch with us.

At this stage, the enlightened entrepreneur has another idea! Their idea is to put an engine (systems) into the car alongside some fuel (cash). Ideally, before they have been pushing the car for too long and have no passion left in them.

Savvy entrepreneurs then obtain some funding; they hire their A team and build the engine (the systems and processes). This process takes time and discipline; however, the enlightened entrepreneurs know that they need to do this or find their business becoming tougher to operate and may even fail. The most enlightened of these will use a business building expert to help them develop the systems. That's typically where we come in as consultants and mentors.

Once the systems have been built, we switch on the ignition of our freshly made engine. The engine fires up, and away we go. Well, with a few coughs and splutters!

At first, the engine is often quite feeble (more of a Model T Ford than a modern car), with the engine not firing on all cylinders and needed constant adjustment to keep going. That said, even this ineffective, wasteful, and misfiring engine is better than pushing the car, i.e. running your business without effective solutions and a low level of cash.

Once the engine coughs into life, the business starts to grow. You will begin to grow again slowly at first, and you soon begin to put a smile back on your face, gain back some of your time and some more cash in your pocket.

Question

Where are you on your business journey?

Be honest with yourself and ideally discuss this with your Mentor or coach.

Realising where you are on your business journey is the first stage of working out what you need to do to get you where you want to be.

The next stage; Improving the performance of the Business Engine.

13. The Business Engine

⸺⸺⸺⊙⚓⚬⸺⸺⸺

The next stage involves you improving your engine. The larger you become, the more complex, more effective, and efficient your engine needs to be. Once you have developed the initial systems, this is no time to relax and think that it's all now plain sailing. The systems you need at $500k are very different from the systems when you are at $5m.

When it's just you, the engine can be basic, and innficient does not fire on all cylinders and must be worked on almost daily. As you grow, you must build in improvements within your systems because a successful business is a Porsche, not a Model T Ford and a Porsche needs 450hp super effective engines to keep on growing and keep on scaling.

I know this is a very simplistic picture I am painting here. Still, it is essential that we all get this as early as possible in our business journey and are reminded of it often because even the best of us forgets the basics. This includes me!

The Four Pistons Driving your Business Engine

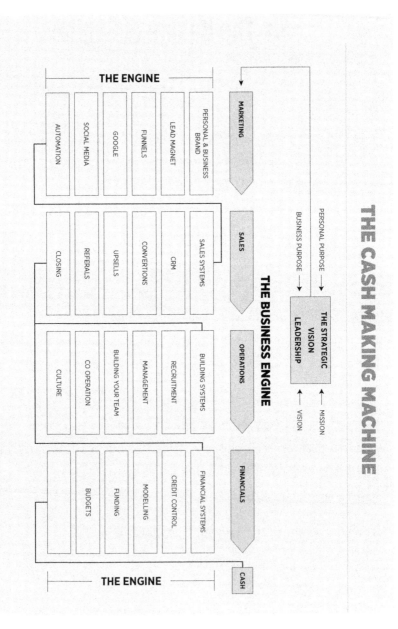

The Marketing Piston

You have a product or service that customers buy from you. If 10 will buy from you then 10,000 will buy from you. One of the significant challenges is to build and refine your Marketing Piston.

In business, we need to generate new leads; these can come from existing or new customers. You will require a process and system for both segments.

We delve into how to generate more leads in another section.

The input for marketing is the market, and the output is a qualified lead that your sales team needs to convert.

Ps. Marketing is not sales, and sales is not marketing. I delve into this within the book.

Some of the processes required to generate leads include:

- Market research and validation
- Marketing strategy and planning
- Lead magnets ie webinars, emails, snail mail
- Funnels
- List generation
- Word of Mouth
- Strategic partnerships
- Affiliates
- SEO
- Google/ facebook/ Youtube adverts
- Marketing campaigns
- Lead qualification
- Marketing automation

These are just general areas, and your business will no doubt be different.

Each process is a process within the marketing process. Once these systems are being built out and tested, lead generation starts to become a tap, to turn on and off as required.

Being able to turn on more or less marketing activity and, therefore, the volume of leads ensures that your sales function operates close to its ideal rate.

Any underperformance of the marketing piston causes stress on the deal flow and leaves the sales team with too few leads, which seriously affects profits and morale.

Overperform and generate too many leads for sales, and you create dissatisfied potential clients because your sales team cannot handle the volume of new leads.

This has a knock-on effect on the pistons, and your engine starts to misfire. When you misfire, you can stall, and you can fail.

The Sales Piston

The input for the sales process is a qualified lead, and the output is a contract or a sale of your product.

The processes in the sales function can include:

- Building' Know Like Trust
- Nurturing
- Proposal writing
- Zoom Presentations
- Follow-ups

- Closing
- Sales automation improvements

You need to take your clients through the sales journey and to optimise the client for the lifetime of the client.

I cover the sales journey elsewhere in this book.

Maximising sales demads numerous systems, and failing to have effective and streamlined systems and procedures means that your sales piston will misfire.

This misfiring has a severe knock on effect on the next piston; Operations, with costs growing and profits plummeting. A misfiring sales cylinder also affects the marketing piston. The marketing team will soon get disheartened if the sales systems do not work as they should.

The Operations Piston

The input for the operations function is after a sale takes place, and the output is an invoice.

The operations function is to over-deliver on the sales promise.

The processes in the operations function can include:

- Carry out the service you have been paid to deliver
- Quality assurance
- Capacity control
- Customer satisfaction
- Recruitment
- Customer complaint
- Operations automation

If your operation's piston is not working correctly and is misfiring, then you will lose clients, you create too many complaints, your reputation will suffer, and profits will plummet. You also piss off the teams operating Marketing and Sales!

The Financial Piston

Lastly, in the business engine, we have the financial operations.

The input for finance is the generation of an invoice from a sale, and the output is cash.

The finance function managers the money, costs, and profit.

The processes of the finance function can include:

- Cash flow management
- Cost control
- Credit control
- Management reporting
- Financial forecasting
- External financial support
- Finance automation

No matter how great your marketing piston is, your sales piston, and even your operations piston, if you operate the finance piston ineffectively, this is a sure-fire way of going bust.

Many business failures have a full order book because all the other pistons worked, and their financial piston failed.

The finance piston is often the last to be considered or most often is simply ignored, and that's a grave mistake that many of us make.

The Four Pistons recap

Each of the pistons needs to be working effectively and efficiently for you to grow and frankly to have a business that runs well.

If any of these pistons are too slow, are less than effective or clogged up then your business will fail and at best it will be really tough to run.

You certainly cannot grow, never mind scale, unless all the pistons are working perfectly and there are very few constraints on the engine.

Solving your Business Engine challenges using the Theory of Constraint (TOC)

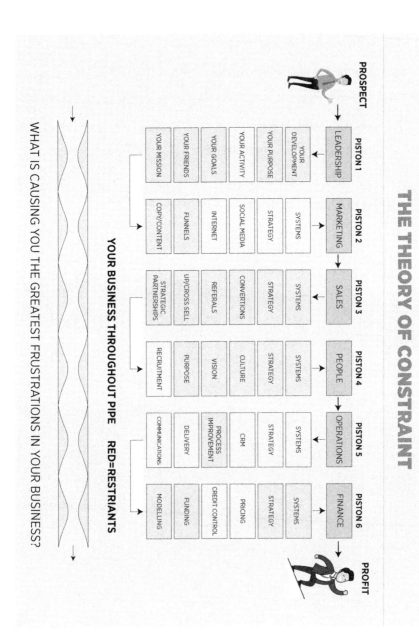

THE THEORY OF CONSTRAINT

WHAT IS CAUSING YOU THE GREATEST FRUSTRATIONS IN YOUR BUSINESS?

YOUR BUSINESS THROUGHOUT PIPE   RED=RESTRIANTS

TOC - The theory of constraint is a very powerful tool that is critical for understanding and putting into practice.

The theory of constraint that was created by Dr Eliyahu Goldratt in 1984 in his book, The Goal.

Understanding TOC can take your business to the next level quickly once you understand the principle and take action. I use this technique all the time in our businesses and the businesses of our clients.

Think of your business as an ever-increasingly wide pipe down which your clients travel. Just like an artery, if you start to restrict the flow with constraints, you will not function correctly, and if these constraints become too severe, you will die.

Ever had a kink in your hose pipe? The water stops flowing. Business is very similar.

Only systemised businesses have a pipe, of course. If a business is not systemised then you have buckets. Think about that for a while....

In a business, you can start to guess where your constraints are by asking yourself, "where am I most frustrated within my business?"

The word frustration is an emotion that manifests itself as a gut feeling, and it's telling you that you're not happy with your result. In other words, poor effects due to constraints = frustration.

So, if you wish to grow, ask yourself the question, What is causing me the greatest frustration in my business right now?

Listen to your body for that natural gut feeling of frustration. What is causing it? You may need to sit down with your coach to bounce this off them.

Using a flipchart or whiteboard, start to write these down. Don't complete this on your own, do this with someone else and ideally your coach or your Mentor.

I would also want you to include your team. Ask them where they are most frustrated.

Some answers I receive from our clients include:

- We are not sourcing enough leads from our website/ LinkedIn etc
- We have spare sales capacity, and we need more leads to fill it
- We need more people in operations because we have too many sales and we are upsetting clients
- We can handle more clients, but sales are not producing the numbers we can handle.
- We need more cash and that's slowing down every area of our business
- We need to improve conversion rates
- We need to improve the average spend per customer
- We need to speed up how fast we are paid.
- We need to improve our recruitment because we keep hiring the wrong people
- We take on new people, and they don't understand how we work quickly enough
- I am too busy to work on the business

Imagine the pipeline of your business again. As the client flows through this pipe, where are the constraints? Ever had a kink in your hose pipe? Instead of a high-pressure jet of water, you have a dribble. Your business is no different.

Reducing the constraints

There are only two or three major constraints in most systemized businesses holding back the business from growth alongside hundreds of minor ones. You need to focus on the most damaging ones first.

Naturally, a none systemised business is not a pipe; it's a bucket.

Use the diagram below to consider where the constraints are within your business. Draw out your business engine and start filling in the boxes and then colour in red where the constraints are.

You could use a colour system for differing levels of constraint.

Then decide which are the most severe and work on those first. Keep in mind that you must retain balance because you don't want too many leads or too many sales.

The other causes for any business constraint are external influence such as a recession - as you cannot control an external influence, you need to look at how you can change something within the business.

Successful businesses use the external constraints to pivot their businesses and don't use them as excuses.

Exercise

Think about where you are on your business journey and be honest with yourself.

Write Out your business engine and work out where your constraints are.

14. Systemise Your Business to Enable You to Scale Successfully.

❧

Without any doubt, you cannot scale a business and maximise your potential unless you have systemised every element of your operation from lead flow, sales, delivery and finance.

The previous chapter focusing on the business engine should bring that home.

When I refer to 'you' I mean your team and you.

We suggest you start with systemising your marketing, lead flow and sales process first; everything else will follow. That's because Sales brings in much of the cash you need to develop the business as a whole.

DO NOT DELAY THIS PROCESS BECAUSE BY DOING SO, YOU WILL REDUCE YOUR PROFITS, INCREASE YOUR WORKLOAD AND RUIN YOUR BALANCE.

We find it helpful that you view your business as a possible franchise. This does not mean that you will franchise your business, just the prototype of a franchise.

This will help you start shaping your business, reducing the current chaos and disorder to such an extent that you could license your model to countless franchisees. You could be confident that each franchise could operate their businesses consistently and profitably without your constant supervision.

You may even decide that franchising your business is the ideal way to grow.

You would be in good company if you did.

All of these companies started from nothing and grew because of systemising their business and expanded through franchising.

- Tax Assist,
- Action Coach,
- Business Doctors,
- TGI Friday,
- McDonald's,
- KFC,
- Burger King,
- Subway,
- Hertz,
- Hilton,
- Pizza Hut,
- Dominos,
- Snap-On Tools

Many of these franchises are run entirely without the owner's input. They are by definition 'A business.'

The franchises where the owner works in the business are still ubiquitous and justifiably so; however, franchisees of this nature, once they have been on our business accelerator program, subsequently start to buy up other franchises and give up their day job!

Let's define business again for you;

A business is a profitable enterprise that operates without you; profits without you.

It is **not** a place where you go to work; that's called a job and not a business.

For example, if you purchased £10,000 in BP shares, would you turn up to the nearest Petrol station and start pumping fuel? Sounds crazy?

When Richard Branson created Virgin Airlines, did you see him flying the planes? Loading the luggage? Checking you in?

No? So why do you do this in your own business?

Once you have created your 'prototype franchise', then it's likely that you would have made a business that can operate successfully without your management input. In other words, the business will now be working for you rather than you working for the business.

This is when you can go on holiday and know that the business carries on without you; bliss!

You can play with your children knowing that you are making money whilst you do.

Back in 2001 I decided to recruit a joint CEO. He had been CFO for a few years and he was a world-class director and leader. I then went on holiday, and when I came back, I was delighted to discover that the business had leaped forwards.

I went on five two-week holidays that year, later took the title 'Director of External Affairs, moved to London and we tripled turnover. All without my day-to-day involvement. The Penny had certainly dropped.

Contrary to a popular myth, it is rare for the founder to be a great MD or CEO.

If you cannot afford a proper CEO yet, then employ one who works with you part-time. I am the 'joint' CEO of around 20 businesses where I spend 1-2 hours a month on each.

Some of you reading this may now be thinking, but I could never let go, or you could be thinking, "there's no one who could take over from my role" Its time to make some changes then.

Warning. If every time you go on holiday, and your business performance improves, then maybe you should go on more holidays? Joking aside, perhaps you should now be thinking of your next venture? That's what I did, and I know hundreds of others who have done this as well.

Systemising your business is naturally quite daunting, and you may wish to ask your coach or mentor to help here. There is no shame in asking for help with systemising your business; we all do it.

You need to start writing down the process and draw a map of the process (or even a Gantt Chart that you will find on ZOHO). Don't worry if this is a little messy; that's to be expected at the outset.

We run one-to-one and group courses on setting up ZOHO because I have never met anyone who set up ZOHO themselves without totally messing up.

Write down the process for every element of your business and this includes;

1. The process to create a prospect (Marketing)

2. The process to convert the prospect to a client, (Sales)

3. The process to input them onto your CRM and to welcome them as a client, (Operations)

4. The process to deliver the service (Operational)

5. The process to collect your payments (Finance)

6. The process to keep in touch (Marketing)

7. The process to gain their custom again and again.(Marketing)

Put these processes into an actual file called your Operations Manual. It will start small and start to snowball until you have a document that you can hand to another, and they can operate your business from it.

Keep the Operation Manual in a prominent place. Add a task for every day that you must spend one hour developing the systems within the manual. This is a very high-level and therefore high value activity.

To make this process work for you, you need to work on the Operational Manual daily, refine it constantly. Take this manual with you everywhere, re-read it and amend it every day.

The act of writing your processes down will make you realise how much chaos you currently create. Solutions to bring order will start filtering into your mind; it's a fantastic process, and you need to start.

Within no time at all, you will find that the writing down of your process helps to calm your business down, and order starts to breaks out!

You will also feel much calmer and less stressed.

When you recruit, recruit for parts of the process that will drive revenue first, even if you feel great. Then you will start to become a systems-based business, one that can grow and scale.

We suggest that you start with your prospect and sales generation process. Writing down the process will help you understand your numbers more readily, and it will also highlight where you can make small changes for considerable increases in sales revenue without needing to spend more money (more on this later)

To support your systems and procedures, you will need to use Customer Relationship Management or CRM. Please don't be tempted only to use spreadsheets because this will severely limit your growth, efficiency, and business value.

To help you create systems for each task in your business, define the following for each system.

1. A title.

2. An objective - explaining the result or outcome the system should produce.

3. A visual diagram, ie a flow, or Gantt Chart - this makes it easier to explain the system and to amend it when you need to.

4. The Tasks - Key steps of the system, who's accountable and the timing.

5. Expectations - performance standards.

6. Resources - the information, equipment or items needed to operate the system.

7. Tracking - the way the system will be measured to ensure that it's working.

To recap:

- Systemise your enterprise so that you are ***systems dependant*** and ***not people dependant***

- Systems are simply structured ways of performing tasks in order to achieve the desired result.

- Prior to starting to systemise your business buy in a CRM package to help carry the new systems. We recommend Zoho to most clients.

- Unintentional or ad hoc systems produce unpredictable and unintended results. A business made up by random systems is successful only by chance, not by design. The business is also likely to fail; quickly.

- A systemised business is worth considerably more when you sell it, than one that is only partially systemised where the founders still have a formal 'day job

Exercise

Write down all the areas of your business that need to be systemised and delegate who is going to actually do the work and by when is the work to be completed.

You may wish to work with your mentor and coach with this.

Then buy ZOHO and have a rummage around yourself then realise you need help because this is a 'high value task that you suck at'

15. Build your Organisational Chart.

Even if there is just you or just you and your 'partner,' you still need to create the organisational chart of your business.

The organisational chart explains each role within your business and then assigns tasks to each position and what each position is accountable for, and to whom.

Top Tip. You may wish to keep a file for all your old organisational charts to look back at your progress. Within a short period, you can look back and see how far you have progressed.

Creating accountability for each of these roles is vital for your growth!

Creating your organisational chart should be a cathartic exercise for you:

- Not least, this process will open up your eyes to the potential of your business,

- The process will also help you realise how many varied roles you currently undertake; and

- You can then ask yourself the question. With most of these jobs you undertake, given a choice, would you employ yourself for the roles?

You will be organising your chart around functions within the business, not around personalities (including yours!); focusing on responsibilities and accountabilities.

The first step is to think of yourself as a shareholder first and foremost. An investor.

While you have this hat on, you are more likely to consider the roles you have in the business, and whether you should fire yourself from some of the roles, you have taken on.

This undertaking is even more critical if you have a 'family' business.

You may find out that your son/ daughter/ mum/ dad have;

1. Too many jobs to do.

2. They may not even be the best person for all or even any of their current jobs.

3. You could let mum/ dad 'retire', make more profit and give them even more income than they were receiving when they 'worked' in the business.

Then it would help if you kept in mind that you are currently also an employee of the business whose primary aim is to enhance shareholder value. This is where you need to ask yourself, "am I the best person for the tasks I undertake? "

If you are honest with yourself, the answer is likely to be no for most of the jobs you undertake.

Then one of you needs to take on the role of Alan Sugar/ Donald Trump in 'The Apprentice' and tell yourself that 'you're fired!'

I came across a company where the turnover was $25m with very little real profit. The CEO also undertook the role of Procurement Director as well as Operations Director; really?

In reality, he was CEO for 0-30 hours per week, the buyer from 0-30 hours, and Operations director from 0-30 hours. I use 0-30 because some months, he would spend zero time in some of the roles. What an idiot because if he had focused his role and sourced superstars for these roles, his business would probably be running at £50m pa and making far more profit.

This scenario was truly crazy when all of these roles needed a full-time executive. The outcome of the short-sighted way of working? Reduced profits, diminished value of the business and worst of all; damaged health because he was 'overworked'. No shit.

They also lost a major contract because one of the plc's buying their products recognised that their business was being operated much like a corner shop and not a business. And for what purpose was the CEO taking on all these roles? Habit and no one connected to the business that was willing to confront this crazy attitude. They should have brought in a Chairman to sort this lunacy.

The CEOs excuse? He told me that it was his 'culture' to 'save money' and to 'work hard'. This chaps family had moved to the UK 70 years ago and the 'culture' he was referring to had long since vanished in the mists of time. He was guilty of believing the bullshit his parents had taught him 40 years ago when he was a young boy.

Sadly, this situation is very common in businesses across the globe and is especially relevant in 'family' businesses.

Back to you.....

You should also have worked out your personal objectives and the objectives of the business before creating the organisational chart.

Below is a list of roles and their basics responsibilities;

CEO (Chief Empowerment Officer) (The 'Executive' bit is a little too pompous for me)

- Accountable for the vision of the business,
- Mentoring the directors and some of the management team to be the best they can be,
- Oversight of the management team and key people in the business to ensure that they are the right fit,
- Enhancing the brand in the market,
- Being the Thought Leader for the business,
- Continually connecting with the key players in your market,

- Reporting to the rest of the board and to the shareholders,
- Should not actually work **in** the business **at all.**

Operations Director

- Accountable for delivering the services promised to the clients by marketing.
- Revises the delivery process to enhance the client experience and reduce costs.
- Reports to the CEO

Sales and Marketing Director (this should be two roles once you reach £1m t/o)

- Accountable for sourcing new customers and finding new ways of satisfying the needs of the customers.
- Creates improvements in the prospect of sales conversion rates.
- Creates new channels and enhances the current media to create an increasing volume of clients.
- Creates strategic partnerships to create deal flow.
- Creates the Sales Strategy and plans.
- Reports to the Operations Director.

Finance Director

- Accountable for supporting Operations, Sales, Marketing, HR and ITC
- Achieving the company's profitability standards.

- Securing external capital (in advance of when it's needed).

- Refines the financial model.

- Financial modelling to optimise the business

- Creates the financial strategies and plans.

- Manages cash flow and predicts cash flow over at least 6 months in advance.

- Creates and then manages the collections process.

- Reports to the Operations Director.

HR Director

- Accountable for recruitment, creating the staff handbook, all training, inductions, leave etc.

- Reports directly to Operations Director

ITC Director

- Accountable for all things tech in the business whether this be the computers, phones, printers, internet, software and to make sure that they work to improve the value proposition

- Reports to Operations Director.

Once you have created a chart (you may need your Coach or Mentor for this exercise), you can start adding in names.

If your business is relatively new to growth, don't be surprised to find that your name goes into a few boxes. Also, keep in mind that while you may currently have a number of these roles, you don't spend any real-time carrying out any of the objectives, do you?

How could you, you already work 10 hour days and your name is now in 4 boxes, each of which needs 8 hours work?….. Let's drill down into this a little;

While your business is small, each role ideally requires 5-10 hours per day to maximise the opportunity, and there are 4 of these roles. So that would equate to around 40 man-hours per day required to ensure that your business is working at its optimum.

If you have taken on these four responsibilities, you can only work 10 hours, yet they require at least 40 hours! So this means that you are only running at 25% efficiency at best.

In principle, if your current turnover is £300,000, by adding these roles in the business and deligating them to experts, in principle you should increase your turnover to £1.200,000. See my point?

Are you starting to realise that you have too many ROLES and your employees (currently **this is you** if you are still the 'worker' in the business) don't really have the time or skill set to carry out their jobs?

Still, wondering why your business is not growing, why you're not making enough profit, why your sales conversions are at 20% and not 60%?

We then suggest that you write a position contract for each of these roles.

This contract defines:

- The outcomes to be achieved,
- The work they are accountable for,
- A list of standards by which the results are to be evaluated.

The position contract is not a job description; it's more of a contract between the employee and the company, a vehicle for everyone to understand who is responsible for what and whom.

It creates accountability.

Again, if this sounds daunting, your Coach or Mentor should be able to guide you.

We believe that the employee should sign these, **and this includes you, the Founder.**

- Defining the tasks

Define the tasks that need to be undertaken in each area of the business.

We suggest that you broke down your business into core tasks:

- Guiding the Business. The entrepreneurial tasks.
- Managing the Staff/ freelancers. Managerial tasks.
- Obtaining New Business. Sales and marketing tasks.
- Transacting the Business. Production and delivery tasks.
- Supporting the Business. Admin, HR and Finance tasks.

Group these tasks together into Jobs, and then you can work out what skill set is required for each job, and subsequently, you can distribute these jobs to the right people.

Keep in mind which jobs need to be prioritised for recruitment and then start recruiting!

Recruiting? Yes, recruiting and recruiting without regard for the cost; work with the value in mind. If your finances are tight, then you may need to borrow some money.

Your first task is to source skilled artisans to handle priority jobs, which will set you partially free from these roles.

If you don't have enough money to pay their salaries, then raise the money by either borrowing it or sourcing an investor.

Do Not Bootstrap.   *Do Not* "Rob Peter to pay Paul"

Top Tip. Do not 'Bootstrap' and try to keep doing these jobs yourself because Bootstrapping is an ineffective method of increasing your profits and building a valued business!!. Raise the further working capital you need by borrowing it.

Bootstrapping is acceptable for the first few months in business to prove the concept, and then it's time to grow up and act like a real entrepreneur.

No business can grow quickly by bootstrapping alone. Period.

Some people call Bootstrapping; Growing Organically. Organic growth doesn't work, so don't do it.

And remember, you don't have a choice if you wish to grow. Bootstrapping and the other oxymoron 'organic growth' will kill your profits, take away your valuable time and diminish your potential. They may even damage your health and family relationships.

Once you have started to fill these positions, your role must change from being the 'worker' to the Manager of the 'workers' and then onto empowering your 'workers' to be the best they can be.

Warning! This is **not** the time to abdicate your responsibilities; you are now the Manager/ Operator and it's time to delegate.

Remember that you have created a system for these roles within your Operations Manual, detailed in the previous chapter. You now need to teach these systems to your new employees.

Do not recruit anyone until you have the process within your new Operations Manual. The process can be rough and straightforward but have a system that you can improve later.

Recruit employees based on the jobs the business needs to prioritise rather than allowing staff to do jobs they are good at yet have little benefit to the company. This is a widespread problem that is likely to kill your business.

In other words;

'Fit people around jobs rather than jobs around people'

When you define the jobs that must be performed by the business to achieve success, before allocating specific people to those jobs, something amazing happens; you can objectively assess whether the priority jobs are being done in the right way to achieve your vision. This makes your job as the Manager so much easier.

Can you see why more holidays, less stress, and more profit are now just around the corner?

You have started to become a proper business that is systems driven and not people driven, the first step to being able to scale.

To ensure that all these systems work together, we strongly recommend that you invest in CRM.

There are several CRM's and many foolishly choose the 'free' systems.

'Free' is hardly ever the ideal KPI to judge the effectiveness of a CRM.

Your CRM will underpin all your business systems, and you need to choose wisely.

If you want a business that is a pleasure to run, then you need CRM.

We recommend ZOHO if you are in a business such as Serviced Accommodation. If you need to understand the system more, book in on one of our courses or come and have a one 2 one. Check this out on www.thegrowthgurus.co.uk/zoho

Exercise

Use this space to build your basic organisational chart

16. Building Specific Job Descriptions to Enable Sustainable Growth

To achieve genuine role clarity and accountability, you must define precisely what's expected in each job.

Your organisational chart goes some way to fostering coordinated, organised action in the pursuit of your vision.

The chart will identify the various jobs that need to be undertaken and then assign them to people, which helps create role clarity and accountability.

When managers and staff are clear on the jobs they are accountable for, they tend to be much more focused, more efficient, and far more productive. This is likely to result in an improvement in morale, performance, profits and value. **People yearn for clarity.**

While the organisational chart is vital, allocating a job to someone and then hoping for the best isn't enough. This is what most businesses 'do,' and you don't want to be like most businesses, do you?

Each job description will include an explicit statement of the results that are to be expected. This removes limitations found in a typical job role. The document is not simply a to-do-list of tasks; it's an agreement to assume accountability for defined results.

This enables managers and the staff members to see their roles in the broader context of the business as a whole, which is likely to impact motivation and commitment.

The Composite Parts of the Job Description.

Job Objective

For a sales agent, the main job objective could be to;

1. Increase the number of opportunities/ leads
2. Increase the channels available that create a deal flow of leads
3. Increase conversion rates,
4. Increase yield per client,
5. Increase number of repeat sales,
6. Increase number of quality referrals,

Targets

A way of measuring whether the objectives are being achieved which includes tangible and quantitative targets.

Tasks

The specific tasks or activities the job

Exercise

Use this space to start building your job role and job roles of your fellow business owners and your closest team.

You may wish to ask your Mentor or coach to work with you on this.

17. Accountability

Being Accountable is the scary bit because creating Accountability means that you will start seeing exactly what is happening in your business. There will be no hiding places!

Being Accountable also almost guarantees that your business and your profits and wealth will skyrocket.

As human beings, we often shy away from seeing reality, so I don't blame you if the prospect of full Accountability fills you with dread.

You will know daily:

- What's in your bank account (Scary at first)
- What your cash flow is likely to look like for the next few months (oh my god, this will give you a heart attack the first time you do this)
- What's in your sales pipeline, and what should be removed.
- Who is doing what and how well they are doing it. (its amazing how much slack there is in most businesses)
- What clients do you need to get rid of and avoid in the future. (watch your happiness levels shoot up)
- What elements of your business are making money and which ones are not. (the results usually comes as no surprise)

Let's admit it; you have probably spent most of your time avoiding knowing the facts and being accountable to them. Don't worry, that's human nature!

However, remaining ignorant of the facts is far from ideal if you wish to build a profitable, high growth and sustainable business.

The great news is that **you will** love this transparency because this transparency and Accountability will allow you to grow your profits and wealth. You will also be able to take more time out of the business. Once you have taken the plunge.

Think about it. Currently, you are driving your car in thick fog, with no idea how much fuel you have left, no idea what direction you are going, and with parts of your vehicle not working correctly.

Once you introduce Accountability, your direction will now be crystal clear, and you will be able to enjoy the drive reassured that your targets and goals are all now clearly in view and you are on target to hit them…

It is vital to have this level of transparency, insight, and Accountability to grow sustainably and quickly. *Vital!*

Of course, much of this is made possible with technology such as Zoho and Xero.

Warning! Not adopting CRM and an accounting package will severely damage your profit, prospects, and the ultimate value of your business.

Most of your competitors will be using CRM such as ZOHO, which will help them out compete you.

IMPORTANT: A CRM and an Accountancy package are no longer a luxury; they are a necessity.

You can stay ahead by ensuring that you employ the services of experts in CRM to ensure that you are taking full advantage of all the CRM has to offer. I suggest that you avoid building your systems into the CRM yourself; you are not the expert. We recommend that you engage a qualified technician to build the systems with you.

It's great that you now have the systems and the platform to be able to operate effectively. However, you must have a "100% buy-in" from all the team, both internally and externally.

"100% buy-in" means that everyone, and I mean **everyone** is fully accountable and fully visible, and this includes you - the Founder.

The great news; You will know the performance of all your salespeople, all your delivery agents, your accounts, etc. No one can hide, nor should they and, in fact, nor should you!

You need to be accountable as well to grow.

You may (will) have to manage a number of your people who don't (won't) use all your systems.

For example, salespeople are typically terrible at completing their part of the CRM if left to their own devices.

Non-compliance will result in both you and your sales director not being able to measure performance.

So, it is necessary to include completing the CRM as a major task that forms part of **everyone's** job spec. This is part of the method to ensure that everyone adheres to the process.

The alternative? Relying on people to do this instinctively will result in your systems becoming increasingly less effective. You need to be tough on this subject if you want to succeed.

Keep in mind that you will receive a steady stream of suggested improvements and one of your team 'must own' this beneficial information.

Systems implementation is **vital** to your success, so we suggest that you engrain these rules within your culture.

It is vital that using the CRM to input everything becomes the norm that everyone expects.

Using the CRM properly will ensure that your people do this naturally, and you don't need to police them.

Regular Meetings.

We encourage our clients to hold two different types of meetings to engrain the systems into their culture and ensure their teams work together effectively.

- **Regular Team Meetings.**

It would be best to meet with your sales team once per week to review their progress against targets. Regular team meetings are a great time to plan the next few weeks and ensure that everyone follows the systems, such as inputting sales activity and clients' interventions onto the CRM.

These sales meetings are also an ideal venue for your team to make suggestions to improve the systems.

- **Weekly Individual Meetings.**

It would be best if you met every week with everyone who reports to you. Likewise, all of these people should meet with their people who report to them weekly. Individual meetings can be used to encourage and coach your people on their performance. You may need to learn coaching skills, and you may also need to learn how to run effective meetings. A great coach and your Mentor can help you with these.

- **Join a Mastermind Group**

Accountability is mission-critical, and nothing beats being accountable to people whom you cannot fire.

A Mastermind group of your Peers who meet regularly can enable you to garner the opinion of your peers on your ideas and challenges. These groups are also critical for Accountability.

If you commit to attaining certain milestones or goals and inform your Peers in the group, you are very aware that you need to have reached this milestone at your next meeting!

I have seen this work thousands of times over the years.

The Growth Gurus has Mastermind Groups that you can join, and they will hold you accountable!

To enquire about our Mastermind Groups just email info@ thegrowthgurus.co.uk

To Recap

- Every recurring task is a system, and you have two choices; either hold people accountable for them or rely on chance. There is no middle ground.

- World-class systems demand that you create a culture of Accountability where everyone knows that using the systems and procedures is mandatory.

- There are two parts to your accountability strategy.

- Ensure that your systems are implemented into your CRM and accounting package.

- Hold regular meetings with your people as a team and on a one-to-one basis.

- Keep in mind that these meetings are fertile ground to work out improvements that can be made to your systems.

Exercise

Write down what you are going to do now to bring about more accountability immediately.

Then add this to your task list on ZOHO or whatever CRM you use.

Not got CRM? Then get it today so you can get your s*it organised.

18. The Business Plan

E very business needs a constantly updated, living, and breathing business plan.

Without a Business Plan, you are very unlikely to reach your full potential, you will make life hard for yourself, and the chance of failure is pretty close to 100%.

"In preparing for battle, I have always found that plans are useless, but planning is indispensable." Eisenhower

There are two main parts to an effective business plan, and they are equally indispensable.

- First of all, you must have a clear sense of what you want your business to become.

I call this the Strategic Objectives.

- Then you will need a well-considered plan of how you are going to get there.

I call this your Strategic Execution.

Another way to look at it is this;

It is almost impossible to create an effective action plan if you don't know where you are going.

And

A clear vision is worthless without a practical action plan to make it happen.

Your Strategic Direction and Execution can, and I believe that it should, be broken into ten mission-critical steps:

1. **Your Purpose**

   Why you exist. What kind of impact do you want to have?

2. **Your Values**

   What attitudes or behaviors are critical to achieving your purpose?

3. **Your Vision**

   What will the future look like when you have fulfilled your purpose?

4. **How do you Differentiate from others**

   What factors will distinguish you apart from the crowd and underpin our brand proposition? What is your niche?

5. **Your Strategic Objectives**

   What your areas of focus must be to achieve your vision

6. **Your Measurements for Success**

   How you will measure your performance in 1,2,3,4 and 5 years

7. **Where you are Today**

   What are the current strengths, weaknesses, opportunities, and threats? If you want an honest answer to this, ask your Mentor.

8. **Your Strategic Projects**

   What you will do this year to hit your targets

9. **Your Action Plan**

What specific actions are needed this Qtr...six months, year.

10. **A Consistent Progress Review**

How you will measure progress.

Identify your Strategic Objectives.

As part of your business planning, you need to define several strategic objectives for the business over the next five years in order to achieve the big picture vision.

For example, here is an objective of mine for the next five years.

1. To help 1 million small business owners to become financially independent and free.

- Strategic Execution; Components.

Once you have completed your Strategic Objectives, you need to define tangible success measures for each strategic objective to crystal clear the goals.

We would then encourage you to complete a full SWOT analysis to assess your business's current state and enable you to lay the foundations for informed decision-making about how you are going to move from where you are now to where you would like to be.

The SWOT will enable you to identify several projects to focus energy on for the current year. You could then map out a detailed action plan for the next three months. There should also be a quarterly review with the entire management team, your coach, and your Mentor.

We conduct this exercise monthly.

Your Strategic Direction and Execution should be broken into ten mission-critical steps:

1. **Your Purpose**

    a. Why do you exist? What kind of impact do you want to have?

2. **Your Values**

    a. What attitudes or behaviors are critical to achieving your purpose?

3. **Your Vision**

    a. What will the future look like when you have fulfilled your purpose?

4. **How you Differentiate from others**

    a. What factors will distinguish you apart from the crowd and underpin our brand proposition

5. **Your Strategic Objectives**

    a. What your areas of focus must be to achieve your vision

6. **Your Measurements for Success**

    a. How you will measure your performance in 1,2,3,4 and 5 years

7. **Where you are Today**

    a. What are the current strengths, weaknesses, opportunities and threats?

8. **Your Strategic Projects**

    a. What you will do this year to hit your targets

9. **Your Action Plan**

    a. What specific actions are needed this Qtr…..six months, year.

10. **A Consistent Progress Review**

    How you will measure progress.

- Create your Business Model to be able to create your Business Plan

There are several tools you can use to create your business plan however, before you start, we suggest that you initially spend time developing your model using a Business Model Canvas.

Alexander Osterwalder originally introduced the Business Model Canvas. There are several variations on the theme, and you may wish to ask your coach or Mentor to find the ideal version for you.

The canvas is a one-page overview that lays out both

1. what you do (or want to do), and

2. how you go about doing it

The Canvas then enables structured conversations around management and strategy by laying out the crucial activities and challenges of your enterprise and how they relate to each other.

This visual format, first introduced by Osterwalder and Pigneur, is helpful for both existing and new businesses. Existing businesses can develop new initiatives and identify opportunities while becoming more efficient by illustrating potential trade-offs, redundant aspects of the business, and aligning activities.

New businesses can use it to plan and work out how to make their offering real.

The individual elements prompt thoughts within the different activities or resources, while the capability to have the complete overview encourages fresh perspectives and ideas about how those pieces fit together.

The Business Plan Canvas also helps to keep group discussions more focused and bring everyone onto the same page.

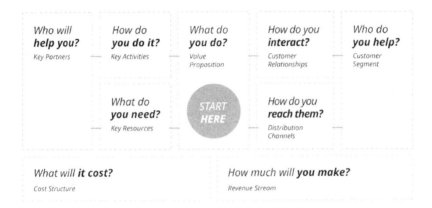

The above is similar to the canvas offered by the Business Model Canvas.

To make a Business Model Canvas, the easiest way to start is by filling out what you do. This helps keep the focus on your primary goal as you fill out the other building blocks of the canvas. From there, you can build on that goal and see how it can be achieved by adding details about the other activities and resources you have.

You may need your coach or Mentor to help with this.

Start from a blank canvas and add notes with keywords to each building block of the canvas. If you use 'sticky notes' for this, you can move ideas around as you fill out each building block in the canvas. You may want to colour-code elements related to a specific client segment.

However, be careful not to fall in love with your first idea and instead sketch out alternative business models for the same product, service, or technology.

You could even practice and learn new ways of doing things by mapping out new/innovative business models that you admire or come across.

Once you have built your ideal model, you can then start with your business plan.

We suggest that you use one of the many template business plans available. You may also find it beneficial to use your coach to create the actual plan.

If you wish to raise funds, then many providers will need a business plan.

We believe that building your Business Plan for a specific funder will require guidance, and we offer business planning support.

To Recap

- Read, study and utilise the Business Model Canvas book and other material to build out your model before attempting to build your Business Plan.

- Keep in mind the recipient of your Business Plan. The Plan for a Start-Up Loan is very different from the plan for a $1m investment into your business.

- Seek out professional help when building your model and Business Plan.

- There are two primary components of an effective business plan:

- A clear sense of where you are going (strategic direction); and

- A well-considered plan for how you are going to get there (strategic execution)

Exercise

Print out 10 business model canvases, spend quality time with your team and mentors, and coach to map out your model.

Don't be surprised when you find that the model you create looks and sounds nothing like the one you have today.

Also, keep in mind that you can create models for different stages in your business, just as with life.

19. Culture Eats Strategy for Breakfast

Your purpose is an excellent way to explain why your business exists.

Your Values represent the beliefs, attitudes, and behaviours essential to fulfilling your business and personal purpose and creating your culture.

Your values form the foundations for your culture because your values serve as a practical guideline for your team's attitude and behaviours.

We would encourage you to nurture your desired culture because this will underpin your brand and how your team works with your clients. This is also likely to lead to higher profits and valuation of your business when you come to sell.

Having the ideal culture is one of the most crucial aspects of growth. There is a phrase in Silicon Valley: 'Culture eats strategy for breakfast....'

In short, you need to define your culture or it will define you, and that seldom ends well.

You will need to decide on your values based on what is important to you, your team, and your business. The following are 8 values we have at The Growth Gurus. Your values are your values. You may wish to consider retaining anything from 3 to 8 values to be effective.

Here are the Growth Gurus values with a brief explanation:

1. **Going beyond what is expected.**

   All of our people take a personal interest in our client's personal and business growth, and we all proactively help out whenever we can.

2. **Trust.**

   Our people value trust very highly because we constantly endeavour to remain a trusted advisor to our clients for 20-40 years plus. Building trust is pivotal to this.

3. **Adaptability.**

   We empower all of our people to focus on an excellent outcome for our clients and we encourage everyone to use their initiative.

4. **Innovation.**

   We send everyone to regular innovation training events to ensure they realise that everyone should innovate, and it's often the simplest of things that can change the lives of millions..

5. **Quality.**

   It is essential that we get everything right the first time and when we don't, to put it right quickly and with no fuss.

6. **Professional.**

   All our people are well organised, punctual and respond promptly.

7. **Fun.**

   Let's not forget that business is supposed to be fun!

8. Honesty.

Often clients are overly optimistic about their business, and part of all of our roles is to ensure that we are as honest as is practical so we can start from the actual position.

Again, these are just an example of our values, and you need to define your own.

Or do what most of our clients do and take the above list and pretty much copy it. Go on; we don't mind!

Once you have shared your values with your team and your staff, you will spend far less time micro-managing people because staff will start to think and act in ways that align with these values.

If you have anyone in your team who strongly opposes your values, you may consider them a 'bad egg' and deal with them accordingly. Time to implement your HR policy, perhaps?

At the age of 23, for the only time in my life, I was fired. Why? I did not fit well within their culture. I had to agree there. The company was being run along the lines of 'Wolf of Wall Street,' and it just wasn't for me.

Naturally, your HR can utilise your values to ensure that you only recruit people who are likely to fit your culture.

You may benefit from your coach's and mentor's input to work on your culture.

Exercise

You use this space to write out your values with a brief explanation, as
I did for our business.

20. Your Vision Becomes Your Reality.

The next stage is to define your Vision for your business.

Your Vision should be what the future looks like once you have fulfilled your purpose. It answers the question; where would you like to be in 5 years…

We all need to set ambitious goals, especially ones that are so huge they embarrass us. Once you know what you are aiming for, you can focus your energy on achieving your goals.

The critical three parts to defining your Vision are:

1. Define your Business Niche.
2. Give Yourself Stretch Goals.
3. Set Time Limits.

1. Defining your Business Niche and then Niche within this Niche.

Your Niche is the intersection between who your customers are, your products or services, and where you will offer it (geographically)

First of all, you need to define your target market. Think laser-focused on a specific area to direct your energy and resources. Think of your efforts as being narrow and deep rather than broad and shallow. Being everything to everyone is likely to end badly.

For example, Serviced Accommodation is a significant niche for us. Serviced Accommodation has been around for 2000 years, but the sector is now starting to disrupt the hospitality sector. It's a super niche with probably less than 200,000 people in the world operating a Serviced Accommodation business seriously, and within the next 5 years this may increase to 1m. So, within hospitality, this represents less than 1% of the entire hospitality 'heads on beds market; it's tiny. That said, focusing down on the Niche of niches can pay off because you become super knowledgeable about that one group.

We have many clients who are super Niche within this Niche.

For example, Serviced Accommodation is a large and growing market in London, but it still represents less than 1% of all stays in London.. One of my clients has created a micro niche with the Niche of just focusing on wealthy Russians. His units are decorated to Russian taste (whatever that is), and the homes feel like a home from home. The result of focusing on less than 1% of the market in London? He charges almost double the rate his contemporaries do, and his occupancy is sky-high. He spends nothing with Online travel agents such as Airbnb and Booking.com, with all his business coming via his website and referrals.

He also makes money providing extra services that he knows his clients will need. He makes a tidy amount from 'close protection' from restaurants he recommends because they all pay him a commission.

You may already be attracting a specific type of client however, I would like you to think about your ideal client because it's unlikely that most of your current clients fit your perfect model.

Think about the types of clients you really love working with, and this may be 5-10% of your current client base. Don't stress about this; it's common to discover that your ideal clients and current clients are not the same.

You could be a finance broker, and you love dealing with clients who need to raise development funds from $500k to $50m. Yet, the bulk of your clients are one-man bands asking you for loans of $20k. The latter frustrates you, and the former delight you.

Imagine if you were working solely for more prominent developers and no longer had to work with smaller ones!

Create your micro Niche within a niche.

Once you have your target market defined and provide your services effectively, you can then consider other target markets.

Facebook is an excellent example. Zuckerberg focused his efforts on the uber Niche of Harvard students only being able to join Facebook. He then added Yale when Harvard was working. He then added all of the Ivy League colleges in the US before the premier Universities such as Cambridge and Oxford in the UK. He was then able to open out to everyone.

If he had tried to attract the whole world, then he would have failed. He focused on his super tiny Niche.

Think about the here and now and then consider your Niche in 5 years.

Your coach will help you refine and define your current Niche and how this will change as you grow.

We suggest you use your coach because this is one of the many areas of your business where you need an external perspective.

It's way too easy to become emotionally attached to your current market, and the leap into micro niching can be scary, but it's almost always worth the risk.

2. Creating a Stretch Goal

We need you to predict the future and then write it down so that it motivates you and the team. To really inspire your team, your goals need to be more than just numbers, i.e., "to reach £5m in net revenue."

Be clear, specific, measurable, and, of course, engage in a series of stretch targets.

Don't forget to set personal goals and keep your core values in mind when selecting these. Remember to set your personal goals first. Your business goals should reflect your personal objectives, not the other way around!

As with your business goals, your personal goals need to inspire and create motivation, so while you should have several financial goals, you will need several goals that add value to others.

3. Creating Short-Term Goals.

Short-term goals for 12 and 24 months are ones you can envisage happening with your current assets and resources.

We would always recommend that you worked with an excellent coach to help you with goal setting.

4. Setting a Time Frame.

You now need to set a time frame to achieve the stretch goal.

Many people set goals for 3 to 5 years; however, we also suggest that you set goals for far into the future. Your very long-term goals require thinking way beyond your current capabilities and resources. It focuses you and your team on being visionary rather than just strategic.

> *"The people crazy enough to think that they can change the world are the ones that do."*
>
> - Steve Jobs

It's now your, and your team's job to create the strategies and plans to achieve these goals.

There are plenty of resources available to help you with goal setting, and you may benefit from using your coach or mentor.

Exercise

Use this space to define your Niche and to build your ideal business client avatar.

Use this space to consider all the extra things you can do for your client's experience, some will create income, and some will not.

21. Growth Demands that you Differentiate your Business from your Competitors

To achieve your vision, you will need to appeal to your target market to the extent that they prefer your products or services over your competitors' offerings.

First of all, you need to ascertain what drives your clients to buy a service such as yours. This means that you must deeply understand their needs on an emotional level.

If you don't fully understand your customers' needs, your marketing collateral, i.e., your website, LinkedIn personal site, social media, brochures, sales pitches, etc., is likely to miss the mark.

Your products or services will also not sell too well because, without truly understanding your customers' needs, all you are doing is selling a product that **you** like. Most people don't like what you want, never mind your target market.

Remember the client I mentioned earlier who sells to Russians? He owns this 100% and is reaping the rewards.

Do you know why your ideal clients buy your services? Have you ever asked them what they find necessary? If you did, you might be a little surprised by what they felt was the most important.

You now need to identify which of the clients' needs you are better at meeting than anyone else. By doing so will truly differentiate your business from others. Or you create the differentiation like our Russian client.

Ask yourself the question; what is the unique value you bring to your market? It would be best if you refined the answer in a clear, compelling, and verifiable way.

Many businesses then capture this in a Brand Promise. This is a phrase that summarises the compelling promise you are making to your target audience. You could even use this to create a 'strapline' or slogan.

At The Growth Gurus, we have a couple that we use:

Helping you to grow a successful business, a real sense of fulfillment and considerable personal wealth while having fun in the process.

Helping you achieve financial freedom within 3 years

Simple and to the point.

You can discover what your clients find essential by asking them. An unusual concept this if you are British; asking the customer what's important to them.

Don't just email them. Set up a zoom call or face to face and question your best clients. This might cost you lunch, but the insights into what your service should be offering will be invaluable.

Be very careful here, though, because Ford once said, "If I'd asked my customers what they wanted, they would have asked for faster horses.'

Exercise

Use this space to explore what are your client's most important needs.

22. Reflection; Learning from our mistakes.

S uccess is a lousy teacher; we only truly learn and progress when we are challenged.

We make mistakes, period. However, learning from these mistakes is a skill that can turn every failure into a success.

The trouble is that most of us went through schooling that punished making mistakes, and so we deep down fear making mistakes to such an extent that we avoid many things in business to avoid making a mistake.

Our ability to learn, grow and succeed depends mainly on engaging in the process of self-reflection.

Introspection

First of all, find a quiet place away from everyone and everything. In winter, my local medieval church and summer, my local graveyard are the places where I go to reflect and identify and become aware of my contributions to an apparent 'failure'.

Remember what a failure is: simply a lesson, a lesson to teach you patience, humility and that there is always a better way.

There is nothing wrong with failing; nothing.

I then go through the following process:

- Focus on the unsuccessful experience.

- Attempt to recall your thoughts, emotions, and behaviour.

- Think of the outcome you wanted to achieve.

- Self-diagnose why you were unable to achieve the outcome you desired by creating ten answers to the question 'I failed to achieve this outcome because?'

- Select the top 3 or 4 of the more significant and then ask yourself, "What can I learn about myself from this explanation?"

- Keep in mind any unhelpful thought patterns or stories you are telling yourself and any personality traits or habits you have picked up.

Articulate

Secondly, you then need to articulate how you contributed to the situation](failure), both in writing and orally

Commitment

Next, commit in writing and orally what you will do differently when faced with similar situations in the future.

Use a coach

Finally, we appreciate that this may be challenging to complete until you have practiced time and time again. At first, you may wish to use your Coach. I still do.

What would take you hours or even weeks they should be able to accomplish in an hour or two.

Exercise

You have just taken ownership and full responsibility, and this will help you to move mountains.

Think of a recent 'failure' and run through the process of self-reflection on this page

23. Increase Revenue from Sales First.

Scaling the volume of clients you serve is vital for growth, so is finding more ways of helping the clients you already have.

It would be best if you also considered the most effective channels for promoting your product or service.

As each sales channel is introduced and then improved upon, you may wish to consider adding other media until your leads, and eventually, the sales come from many channels.

To ensure that you know what is working, what is not, and the costs of each, you will need to channel all activity and results through CRM. To do otherwise is foolish.

If you want to increase your sales, we believe that nine broad strategies can work with any business. It does not matter what sector you operate in; the rules apply to everyone with a business.

As you sit down and plan your sales goals, here is some food for thought and ideas for you and your team to play around with.

Thoroughly assessing and then incorporating these strategies within your business is not a one-hour process. You should plan to take two full days with your team and coach to evaluate where you have been over the last year and forecast and plan for the next three to five.

Ten Strategies.

1. Buy a business.

2. Become a Key Person of Influence

3. Write a book

4. Systemise, systemise, and the systemise even more

5. Increase the number of prospects.

6. Improve your sales conversion rate.

7. Increase the buying frequency.

8. Increase the average transaction amount.

9. Increase your average profit margin.

10. Increase the lifespan of your client.

Even modest improvements in any of these nine areas will yield substantial, compounding sales performance results.

Implementing and then improving 4-9 by 25% should increase your profit by around 300%.

By implementing 1,2, and 3, your prospect flow will likely jump by far more, and your sales conversions will go through the roof.

Buying a business can double your sales in an instant.

Before you decide to spend more money on creating more prospects, please consider these ten strategies.

This chapter will dig down a little into each area to help you investigate how you can incorporate these strategies into your business. If you have a coach, you may wish to ask them to work with you on implementing these strategies.

1. Buy a Business

The quickest and least costly way to grow your sales? Buy a business or two, or three.

Buying a business can take you from £100k per annum to £200k within weeks. If you buy a few more businesses, this could see you grow by a further £500k, Or if you are already at £5m, you could grow to £15m within a matter of months.

Where you are at the moment does not matter.

If you are already at £1m and you have taken 10 years to get there, you could buy another £1m business within weeks. Once you realise this, it can hit you hard. It certainly did for me. I spent 10 years building a business to £15m, and I could have done the same in 3 years if I had thought more like an investor and not an operator.

The best part is that buying a business may not even cost you any money upfront.

In many cases, you may need to fund some of the purchases. However, there are plenty of strategies to recover this money.

Then it's a case of rinse and repeat.

Buying other businesses is an important subject that I have created an entire section for you to read.

2. Become a Key Person of Influence

If you become a Key Person of Influence within your niche, your leads and sales will skyrocket. Daniel Priestley has written an excellent book on the subject called 'Key Person of Influence .' This book is on our 'must read' list you will find later in this guide.

We all know of people in specific sectors who are effectively superstars. They earn considerably more than everyone else in their industry, and they have achieved this by becoming a Key Person of Influence.

For example, there are thousands of business coaches in the UK and US. Many of them are very good, and most are not. But the ones with the most sales, such as Grant Cordone, Gary V, Mel Robbins, or Tony Robbins, earn $100m+ each plus per year because they are Key Persons of Influence.

I like Gary V and Tony Robbins for the record, but in my humble opinion, Grant C is full of s*it.

There are plenty of more effective coaches than these guys, but their sales are less than 0.01% of the key persons of Influence. Why is this? Are their services more or less effective; yes and no.

The significant difference is that these guys have become Key Persons of Influence, and business comes to them much more quickly and on a larger scale.

By way of an example. In 2003 my board and I were on a yacht from Nice to Monaco to watch the Formula 1. Several members of the press called wanting a comment on the collapse of the most significant player in our market. 3,500 lost their jobs, and the company had just sent a text that morning firing them all. Why did they ring me? Because I was the Key Person of Influence in that market.

To my delight, I was also called by the Insolvency firm brought in to deal with the collapse. They asked if we could come in and help with the 'runoff' This led to a £150,000 per month contract that lasted 18 months.

Were we looking for this work? No, they came looking for me because I was a 'Key Person of Influence.'

These days it's so much easier to become a KPI, and you can benefit from this even as a 'small' business. You can become a global KPI and have an international business with just a few of you.

I would estimate that becoming a Key Person of Influence would increase prospect conversions by at least 50% and increase your lead flow by 10,000% or more.

Rather than explain the method in this book, I recommend reading Daniel's excellent book and watching his many Youtube videos.

3. Write a Book

Writing a book that resonates with your potential clients is likely to dramatically increase the volume of leads you produce and, more importantly, increase the likelihood that they convert to a sale and then buy your stuff.

Writing a book enables you to have a national and even global reach that no other route to market can give you.

Many of your prospects won't even buy, never mind read your book and will buy from you because you have written a book!

When this book was in the manuscript stage, we would send this to prospects, and our conversion rate tripled, and most of these entrepreneurs asked about more of our services.

Those who do read your book are far more likely to start to trust you and to feel emotionally connected to you, and then buy into your service.

As Daniel Priestley puts it, a book or books are the foundation of your 'product ecosystem'.

I would estimate that if your prospects were aware that you are an author, your conversion from prospect to clients should increase by at least 10%. If they read your book, then the conversion rate should skyrocket.

Your prospects will be able to understand you as a human being as well as the ways you can help them. It's even better than having a meeting because they can learn about you in their own time.

Writing a book does not take as long as you think, and it's much easier than you may be imagining. I made the error of not using a business book writing coach. That would have saved me countless hours. Apparently, this book is five times as long as it should be, and I started while my youngest was in the hospital 5 years ago.

4. Systemise, systemise, and then systemise your sales process some more!

Most business founders will tell you they need more leads, and they are often very wrong in this opinion.

The perceived need for more leads is why so many companies sell you products or services to source you more leads or more sales. Don't get me wrong; these methods are typically essential; for example, LinkedIn is fantastic at producing leads. But without a sales system, there is no point in scaling these channels without converting these leads.

I've even found a few of our clients who needed fewer leads. Some businesses may need fewer leads because they burn their leads, which costs money and damages reputation. These businesses don't tend to have the capacity to take on the new business.

With our peer review world, this can be disastrous for your reputation.

There is so much more to running a company than simply focusing on leads and sales. If you want to stay in a one-man-band working 60 hours, then carry on; you will fail eventually and struggle for possibly years before failing. If you're going to grow your sales, you need to develop your systems first.

You need to have;

1. A sales strategy and plan
2. Systems to record and manage the deal flow and customer journey
3. Capacity to handle the inquiries properly
4. Effective management of your people
5. Customer-focused Customer service
6. More than enough working capital, so you don't run low on cash

When you obtain leads and hopefully convert those to sales, the sales only stick if you can deliver for your customer.

Then you can also increase your repeat sales by having the systems in place that underpin this process.

A customer can smell that you are running a madhouse and not an efficient machine. Chances are they won't come back, and worse still, they might write about it on LinkedIn, Facebook, or Google.

So without systems and the management to deliver your service or product, if you attempt to grow, your company will ultimately slide back to the maximum capacity it has already achieved without being able to retain even one customer more.

If you're currently stuck in this cycle -- Groundhog Day -- it's time to stop chasing more leads for a while and start working on systemising your sales process as well as your business as a whole.

Figure out what areas you need help in, and you should have an idea now that you have completed our business Audit. You can also employ a professional coach, take on a mentor, join a Mastermind Group, or you could even engage a fractional Sales Director.

Once you have figured it out and fixed your systems, your sales will soar, so will your profits, and your time would be better spent with your family than fire fighting.

5. Increase the Number of Prospects:

Currently, how are you generating prospects for your business?

Are you deluding yourself that you are satisfied with the volume of prospects? Do you simply 'hope' that more clients will come to you?

Speaking from experience, "hope" is not a terrible business strategy, and certainly not when it comes to promoting your business to your ideal clients.

If "I 'hope' more prospects come in next month and next year, "… if this is your strategy – stop it now and get some help!

Let's focus on how you could generate more prospects.

- A Website

If you want your business to be taken seriously, you will need a Google optimised website built by professionals. Don't build your own because it will be shit, and it won't work as it should.

If you deal with other businesses, you must have a professional website or say goodbye to 90% of your potential clients. No professional likes to do business with someone who looks like an amateur.

Can you imagine attending a meeting in the real world, producing your business card, and there is no link to your website on there? They are going to think that you are a total amateur. Wave goodbye to that potential deal.

For example, for a B2B serviced accommodation provider, Let's say you walk into a business and you want to encourage them to book your Serviced Accommodation. Are you going to ask them to visit Booking.com or your website? It sounds crazy, but even now, in 2021, there are still fools out there who don't have a website. If.

- Google; the number 1 route to market because it is the market. Virtually all of us use Google to search for absolutely everything!

No matter what service you offer, most people will Google your business, and Google your competition. I mentioned earlier that most product sales are concluded before they pick up the phone, and most of that research is conducted on Google.

We just bought a VW Camper to take my daughters to the beach. I needed several specialist items fitted, so what did I do? I Googled 'VW Transporter specialist,' and up popped a local garage specialising in helping VW Camper owners.

I needed to hire some scaffolding so my decorators could paint the outside of the house. Guess what I used to find a few local businesses? Thats right, Google.

I wanted to change the administrator of my SSAS pension; Used Google.

I could on and on, but I use Google to search for a supplier of some sort or other virtually every day. If you are not found easily and quickly on Google, then you are losing lots of clients.

Google Ads will enable you to compete head-on and at the same level as any company in the world.

On Google, you can be the Heavyweight in your area, and you can compete directly with the big boys.

The great news is that you will see results straight away with **Google Ads**.

Once you have tested Google at a low level, you can scale up or retain the same budget.

The bottom line is, we are all Googling what we need, and your business can take some of that business.

I have heard quite a few horror stories over the years of business owners running their own Google Ad campaigns. Having read through this book so far, I'm sure that you will guess their results? Everyone failed to deliver the cost-effective number of prospects that required compares to the experts.

There are plenty of agencies out there who can help you maximise Google for your business. Just make sure you engage a professional and not some kid working from a 1 bedroom flat in Manila who does Google adverts part-time.

- LinkedIn

If you are in the B2B or professional space, are you using LinkedIn effectively? I doubt that you are because of the 500m users, less than 0.001% are using the platform effectively, and the rest are the consumers of LinkedIn. Are you using a strategy of "hope" like virtually everyone else?

LinkedIn is *the* most powerful tool available to generate a consistent flow of targeted professionals, business owners, and HNW clients. Nothing else comes close. Nothing.

If you use LinkedIn correctly, then your prospect and conversion rates will increase. That's because your prospects can readily find out all about you. They can read your profile. They can read your posts, read your recommendations, and see what you have added to other people's posts. They can feed on all of the content and are then likely to make a buying decision from this information.

If you get LinkedIn wrong and then the converse can happen. A lousy profile, for example, could result in your prospect running to the hills. So, can a lack of Posts.

LinkedIn can work wonders for your business as long as you use it properly. Currently, the chances are probably at less than 0.001% of your potential lead flow from LinkedIn.

What you need to do: You need to find, engage and promote your services to your ideal clients.

You need to source your ideal clients and send out 200-600 personalised invites and /or messages per month to encourage your network to talk to you about your business.

Of course, these are not going to be all your ideal clients. Linkedin doesn't work this way. These need to be connected to your ideal clients so you can grow your network more rapidly with this strategy.

You need to send out 10 to 60 posts per month to your network and repost other people's content. These posts need to be relevant to your audience, posts they will care about.

The Result: Warm, engaged, ready-to-talk prospects direct from LinkedIn

Tap into the LinkedIn experts who manage much of LinkedIn for you. They will often have a unique understanding of what works (and what doesn't!) when engaging prospective clients. That's because they will manage 100s of accounts every day, unlike a LinkedIn trainer who has little real-life experience.

They will continually test, tweak and adjust their approach to your ideal prospects based on their overall experience, feedback, and engagement, ensuring that they will maintain a real-time process that brings you to the best ROI

What you need to do in detail on LinkedIn.

- **You need to optimise your profile.**

You only have one chance to make a first impression. A profile that reads like a CV is not attractive to your prospective clients. Is your profile putting people off from talking to you?

An improved profile will dramatically increase the performance of LinkedIn to produce leads.

Your profile needs to inform your prospect how you can help them within the first few words. Lose them at this point, and you lose them forever. Refining the optimum profile is an ever-changing skill that is best left to a professional.

- **You need to send out 200-600 personalised connection Invitations to your target audience.**

It would be best if you grew your network rapidly. "Your network is your net worth". Tim Sanders.

A proportion of your new network will enquire about your service immediately; however, the prime reason is to increase the audience of your posts that will be full of awesome content that your ideal client is interested in.

- **You need to send professional and personalised follow-up 'thankyou' and 'let's chat' messages to all new connections.**

This action shows your new connection that you are 'polite' and that you care about them. This vital step builds up awareness, confidence, and trust in you, leading to conversations.

A proportion will enquire about your service because of this message.

- **You need to send out up to 20-60 personalised messages per day to your network, encouraging them to talk to you.**

Creating conversations is what LinkedIn is best at; however, this only works due to the massive level of activity that it does for you.

This volume of direct messaging encourages conversations, and these lead to business.

- **You need to create and then send at least 10-60 Posts per month of your content to your network**.

Posting content that is of interest to your ideal clients is critical. Content catches the attention of your ideal clients within your growing LinkedIn network, builds trust, and creates conversations.

Within a short period, your entire LinkedIn network will start to recognise you as the 'go to' person, and this will encourage conversations that lead to new business.

Using LinkedIn effectively is a high-level skill that you are unlikely to pick up during a training course. Secondly, most of the tasks involved are monotonous and require consistency. Ideally, you should delegate these critical tasks to an experienced team member or delegate the job to a professional LinkedIn management company.

The leading player who can manage much of your LinkedIn profile and enable you to focus on the higher value activity is our Linkedin Gurus at www.inlinked.co.uk

I implore you not to fall into the trap of doing all the work on Linkedin yourself. Use a specialist agency to do all the grunt work, and you handle the actual conversations with people who want to talk to you.

- Word of Mouth Referrals:

Referrals can and should be one of your primary ways to generate more qualified prospects.

Referred clients tend to have a much higher conversion rate because someone the prospect respects recommended you.

Do you have a specific sales model in place to encourage more referrals and word of mouth? If you don't, then you need one. A company called Word Of Mouth www.womtwo.com offers training programs for you and your team; well worth the investment.

Do you ask your customers or clients for referrals? Even simple positioning can make a difference.

For example, we recently sent an email to our clients and strategic partners headed 'We love referrals.' We wrote about the specific type of customer we were looking for.

This simple message motivated a number of our clients and partners to start them thinking. All we did was educate them on what type of clients we are looking to serve, and hey presto, five referrals came in, with four becoming clients over the next few weeks with another five signing up over the next month.

This exercise cost around £250 in direct costs and £100 in commission, equating to just £125 per client.

Within this year's marketing strategy, we are targeting two referrals per client per year. We target over 400 clients from referrals in this coming year, and you could do the same.

Let's put that into some perspective.

If you obtain 100 clients this year and you adopt our strategy, this could result in you taking on a further 200 clients within the next 12 months.

We are incentivising our clients with commissions, Ipad's and even a competition where the top prize is a trip to the Monaco F1. The only downside will be that I will be there as well!

Think about how you could encourage your clients, strategic partners, employees to help you to gain more referrals.

It is vital that you guide your clients on explaining the service you offer and how best to make the referral. We prefer an email where all parties are included within the email.

Hi John,

As you know, we are expanding, and ensuring that we do so sustainably, we engaged the services of The Growth Gurus. They continue to support us during the process, and they have suggested several changes that we needed to implement.

One of the changes helped us increase our prospect conversion rate from 10% to 20%, and that tripled my profits without spending any money, which was great.

I have also joined one of their Mastermind Groups, and our business has doubled within the last months as a direct result.

I think that you should have a chat!

John, this is David's number 07521 555 555. (This is not an actual number)

David, this is John's number 07522 555 555 (This is not an actual number)

Please call each other and have a meet-up!

After all, apart from some thought and an email, what is the client's cost? If we have agreed to a commission, we pay this immediately that the referred client engages us. Our clients love receiving their £100 commission cheques!

This exercise will also help your client or customer realise that they can use this process in their business. If they have engaged one of our coaches, they will definitely use referrals to generate more clients!

- Reactivation of 'Lost' Customers:

Do you keep in touch with unsuccessful prospects and customers you have not dealt with for some time?

How about your clients who are no longer doing business with you?

If you can proactively contact the old customers who used to do business with you with a special offer to come back or to keep in touch with them and maintain your relationship, you can always generate 'new' leads.

The fact is that only 3% of people buy on 1st contact, and the majority need 7' touch points' before they trust you enough to buy from you.

The money is in the follow up.

If you wrote an actual letter or email to all your prospects once per 90 days, that's going to cost you less than £4 per year per old lead or customer. If your product or service is of high value, you might consider using a quality envelope and hand-sign each letter. We do this, and it's amazingly effective because the recipient sees that you care enough to write to them and sign it personally!

If you have 500 old prospects on your CRM and sending a letter that costs £1 every 90 days creates five new clients, then the cost of each of these new clients is just £100 each.

You could also include them in your LinkedIn Posts and your blogs. You could also send them interesting and relevant information via LinkedIn using messaging.

If your clients are of low financial value, you could opt for an email with less cost.

Whoever your clients are, you and your coach should devise an effective way to generate new custom from old clients.

Remember this formula

2% of sales happen on the 1st contact

5% od sales happen on the 3rd contact

80% of sales happen on the 5th contact

If you follow people up, you will increase your sales

- New or Improved Services or Products

Do you have any new services or products that you can introduce to current and old customers or even leads who did not buy from you?

If you improve your services or products, how often do you promote these to your current client base?

We believe that you should create a new or revised product or service that complements what you already offer at least every six months.

You could then introduce new products or services to current clients and those who did not buy from you in the past.

Apple, Samsung, Microsoft, and many other world-class businesses use this technique, so why not you?

How many would buy your new or revised product/ service? 10%? 30%? 100%?

Often this can also open up a new target market that can generate new prospects for your business.

Business owners, who didn't have a reason to buy from you in the past, may do so now with your new product offering.

We do bring out new products and services every few months, and it's amazing how many sales we create from leads who were simply not interested before.

We recommend that you use your coach to create the strategy to implement new or revised products or services.

- Become a Thought Leader.

Thought leadership is a marketing strategy used to establish you as an authority in your field to achieve a commercial goal.

Done well, thought leadership needs to improve understanding of a pressing issue or challenges significantly, and often challenges underlying assumptions and received wisdom. Genuine thought leadership often provides both personal (organisational) and altruistic (wider industry) benefits.

Thought leadership marketing is an effective way to demonstrate empathy with clients and drive commercial success through the power of your insight and ideas.

Thought leadership is an integral part of also becoming a Key Person of Influence.

Research into buyer expectations in the B2B sector shows a growing demand for organisations to demonstrate their commitment to their sector.

By sharing insights in your LinkedIn, Facebook, Youtube, and Instagram posts about pressing issues and how they might be addressed. Thought leadership marketing helps you to show how you are adding value. In the process, it starts new potentially commercial conversations with clients and prospects.

Thought leadership is why I spent 1000+ hours writing this book. (I added this once it was finished)

Why is it so essential to ensure that your thought leadership marketing is right? Primarily to cut through the noise, demonstrate expertise and find an effective way to build relationships with prospects.

Buying behavior in B2B has changed dramatically over the last several years, and being a thought leader is one of the primary marketing strategies you need to implement.

Another reason to focus on a niche and then niche within the niche.

According to Google, buyers can be 90 percent of the way through their purchasing journey before making official contact with a service provider, exploring areas such as online research, peer recommendations, peer reviews, and service specifications. Reports suggest that the journey would have been just 5% complete when a potential buyer picked up the phone in 2000.

Many of our larger clients utilise the services of Thought Leadership agencies, and I don't blame them.

Lastly, if you wish to maximise LinkedIn, being a fantastic Thought Leader should produce phenomenal results.

- Paid Advertising:

Paid advertising is still a great strategy …possibly one of the most scalable and one of the most fundamental after buying a business and paid for LinkedIn, Google, Youtube, Instagram, and Facebook marketing.

With organic ranking on Google becoming increasingly harder to achieve and organic page reach on Facebook declining rapidly, both platforms are becoming a pay to play arena.

With the right strategy, paid advertising on social media will be very effective at generating an increasing volume of prospects.

With digital paid advertising, it is easy to track results. Ideally, these results should be tracked through a CRM such as ZOHO, Hubspot, Salesforce.

Many of our clients generate very good results using paid Google Adwords, Facebook ads, Youtube ads, and Linkedin Adverts.

For your ideal Linkedin agency where they can either train you or do most of the 'high value yet you suck at it' activity, then visit www. inlinked.co.uk

There are also other paid advertising options that are likely to make sense for your business to generate more prospects.

I also believe that you would be best served using paid advertising by utilising an expert in LinkedIn, Google and Facebook. If you try to manage these yourself, you will likely not be as effective, and you will probably fail to deliver.

- Organic SEO of your Website

It is becoming increasingly challenging to achieve top rankings for your website keywords. Thankfully much can be done to improve your positioning on the search engines.

A well-managed SEO campaign can be an important way to increase the number of times your website is visited by prospects and the number of prospects you convert from simply a visitor.

I was speaking with a prospective client recently, and he was talking about how "nice" a website they had, but nobody visited it. This is a classic paradox since "If you build it, they will come" does not apply to websites or, in fact, anything at all.

Organic SEO requires work, and you can either learn to do this yourself, employ someone to do this, or engage the services of a professional agency. In the early days of SEO, I believe that buy in the experts, and if you don't have the funds, borrow the money.

While SEO is working in the background, ideally, you should be using Pay per click advertising.

- Strategic Partnerships.

Creating strategic partnerships with companies with aligned values and clients is likely to be an effective method.

Many such partnerships are born out of the referral of work to each other for mutual gain.

For example, we have teamed up with a select group of trainers in a wide variety of markets. We support their clients with the value we deliver, and they supply our clients with the value they provide.

Warning. Be careful when dealing with companies with questionable standards and ethics because their motivation may not be as honourable as yours.

Top Tip Strategic partnerships could also blossom into mergers or even outright purchases of one company by another.

- Strategic Networking:

Be uber smart with your networking. Are you appearing in front of new people and building new relationships every day?

How many more people know about your business today than yesterday? 5? 50? 500?

Attend networking events that are right for your market; you may benefit from BNI, Business Over Breakfast, Shout!, Natwest networking events, networking by The Chambers of Commerce. There are also hundreds of Facebook business groups, LinkedIn' local' groups popping up worldwide.

Attend them regularly, and your prospect volumes should start to increase.

Our average lead flow by one of our Growth Gurus Agencies is 200 leads per year from networking, with 50% converting into clients. The estimated cost over the year is £5000 that equates to a cost per client of £50. If you have written a book, you can at least triple these numbers, and if you have become a key person of Influence, you can 10x these numbers or more.

The main cost here is time, and you are likely to benefit from one of your team focusing on networking events and following up on these leads alone.

You could offer to speak in front of groups in your area of expertise and build relationships. I did this just to practice my' pitch' in front of an audience.

For example, I recently offered to be part of a panel on business growth within Chambers of Commerce in several local cities.

Position yourself as an expert as a Key Person of Influence. Offer your knowledge and insights, even if it is for free, and just watch the eager prospects lining up to work with you.

Effective networking is a skill, and I believe that you would benefit from coaching to become highly competent at networking.

Keep in mind that LinkedIn is also networking; however, the reach and effectiveness will dwarf face-to-face networking, so use LinkedIn as the priority platform.

- Referrer Networks

Referral networks are similar to Strategic Partnerships, and, in many ways, they are.

For example, The Growth Gurus has a referral network of business trainers, accountants, finance brokers, IFA's banks, Chambers of Commerce, insolvency businesses, and many more B2B enterprises.

Many referrers are also clients, and it's common for our clients to refer 4 or 5 clients to us.

The referral networks vary in activity level, and many referrers use The Growth Gurus as an added value product to their offering.

For example, proactive accountants who care about clients may well consider referring their clients to The Growth Gurus if they expressed a desire to grow and did not have the resources or expertise available to them. The referral results in a happy client who is pleased with their accountant for being proactive.

For your business, you need to consider what organisations would benefit from referring to you. They may wish to add value to their relationship simply, or they may also ask for a commission.

To Recap

These are just a few ideas on how to generate more prospects. This shortlist is not comprehensive, but it should give you and your team comprehensive strategies to discuss.

I also believe that you would benefit from an experienced coach to maximise the methods that fit your business.

Exercise

Write down your ideal methods to increase the volume of prospects and list out your proposed strategies to improve your sales conversions.

You may wish to work with your coach. You may also want to speak to our experts.

6. Increase your Conversion Rate.

You and your team must all become experts at converting your prospects into new customers or clients: period!

Simple improvements to the conversion rate can make a huge difference to your bottom line without the need to spend more money on marketing.

Many business owners don't focus enough effort on improving their team's selling abilities, and then to make matters worse, they pay very little attention to their conversion rate. They don't have a system to measure it; they don't track it. Do you?

This can apply to both visitor-to-prospect conversion on your LinkedIn, Facebook, Instagram, website, or place of business, as well as prospect-to-customer conversion rates.

If you're doing all the hard work of generating new prospects and driving people to your Website or contacting you via LinkedIn, then you want to make sure that you are converting as many of them as possible.

Keep in mind that if your conversion rate is currently 10% and you increase this to 20%, not only will you double your turnover, you should more than triple your profit.

Don't forget that if you increase the number of clients you serve, you will also increase your delivery workload and increase the costs associated with delivery. You are likely to experience a need for additional working capital if you increase conversions.

DO NOT RELY ON AN INCREASE IN SALES INCOME TO FUND YOUR GROWTH; USE OTHER PEOPLE'S MONEY.

Naturally, you will also require a CRM system to measure your conversion rates, enabling you to track your performance. Most, if not all, of the systems will let you do this.

I believe that you should work with your coach to focus on all the areas needed to maximise your conversion rates.

- The power of follow-up.

How often do you follow up on an enquiry? If you are like most founders, even with a team of salespeople, you will be losing the vast bulk of sales because you don't have the ideal follow-up strategy.

Here are the raw stats I remember reading somewhere.

- 3% of sales are conducted on the 1st contact
- 5% of sales are conducted on the 2nd contact
- 7% of sales are conducted on the 3rd contact (most salespeople are too embarrassed to try again)
- 10% of sales are conducted on the 4th contact
- 75% of sales are conducted on the 5th contact. Boom!

The follow-up has been studied for years, and there are endless stats to prove how and why a salesperson fails to excel in sales. Many sales are lost right here because the average salesperson does not conduct a follow-up call or email at all. For me, there are three categories of salespeople; Which one do your salespeople fit into? If you are the salesperson, where do you serve?

The bottom 5% or "the order takers." These poor performers lack focus, drive, and wait for instructions from the boss or prospects to call or visit. They put in their time and wait passively all day instead of creating opportunities.

Everybody else – up to 79% are "average salespeople." They make up the bulk of most sales teams. Most lack confidence in their abilities and rarely follow up with a client more than four times after the initial inquiry. They put in more time and effort, but often it's busy repetitive work. Unfortunately, 80% of sales staff contribute less than half the sales or results.

Top performers, or the top 20%, produce 50%-80% sales by sifting through the noise that doesn't matter. They delegate when necessary and have a laser-like focus on results. They know the magic formulas to sales success, including that meaningful and consistent follow-up between 5-12 times pays off.

One of the critical elements of your sales strategy of a systemised follow-up process that your CRM underpins will pay huge dividends.

Then your sales team needs to be focused on understanding the principles of the follow-up.

- Clear messaging and call to action on your LinkedIn, Post, blogs, and Website:

Is your messaging clear? Do your prospects know what you offer within a few seconds? We spend a great deal on this section because of the value a clear message can bring to your business.

Spend quality time considering your lead statement, and you may wish to engage a marketing expert and your coach to help you with this. I believe that clients are often too close to their service or product to consider their message objectively.

Our messages are simple:

'Supporting the Directors of High Growth Companies to be the best they can be.'

'Helping you reach financial freedom in 3 years or less.'

I strongly believe in using Video within LinkedIn, Facebook, Instagram, and your Website to get your message over clearly. Video is far more effective at converting visitors to clients than just using text.

- Use Video on LinkedIn, your Website, Youtube, and social media:

To supercharge your performance, you will need several videos that promote your message. There is nothing better than Video to convert visitors to prospects; one of the most significant factors in creating new clients.

Try and avoid the new trend of the amateur-style Video where you are taking the Video on your own. Unless you are a one-person operation, you don't want to look like a one-person operation!

Unless you are an expert at producing Video, I would recommend that you invest in training. There are a few trainers available, and our team can point you to one close to you.

The main Benefits of Adding Video on LinkedIn, Social Media, and your Website.

The ability to attract, engage and bring visitors back to your LinkedIn profile and website is critical. If you wish to be noticed and stand out from the noise, videos are an excellent option to increase conversions.

1. **Quickly Deliver Your Message.**

Video is ideal for getting your message across in a format visitors will quickly and easily digest. People are lazy, and Video satisfies our natural lazy nature.

Video should completely replace written content, but it is an excellent complement to your copy; it will strengthen your message overall and help turbocharge the level of visitors who engage with you.

2. Engage Your LinkedIn, Facebook, and Website Visitors.

Video is a great way to bring visitors to your Website through improved search engine rankings, ensure that they focus on your message in multiple ways (visually, audibly, etc.) and ensure that they spend more time on your profile and Website.

Video on LinkedIn and FaceBook will massively increase the reach of your Posts. LinkedIn prefers Video and will boost your posts to many more people. We can send out a text post with a static picture and receive 300 views and a couple of 'likes.' We produce a video on the same issue/ idea, and then this can jump to 3,000 views, a mountain of Likes, and prospect enquiries!

3. Be Entertaining.

We believe that your Video should not just be informative; it should also be entertaining and even funny.

After all, that is how viewers will remember it, share it, and maybe even make it go viral. Wouldn't that be great!

4. Give Your Company a Personality and build your personal brand with Video.

You can claim to be a hip, cool, and fun team who is dedicated to solving your customers' problems and delivering on their needs until you are blue in the face. But we suggest that you use Video to drive home that message.

Try and avoid just telling people about your day. Stick to producing content that your ideal client wants to consume.

5. Strengthen the Bond with Your Visitors.

A great way to strengthen the bond between your LinkedIn profile and your website visitors is to publish videos featuring your people. People love to buy from people they know, or at least that they feel they know.

So we suggest that you introduce visitors to your team through Video.

Whether the videos are employee profiles, process explanations, product demonstrations, or a live delivery of your values, Video is a great way to get visitors closer to you and your company.

6. Stand Out from Your Competition

In a world of "me too" companies, video content is a superb way to differentiate yourself from your competition.

Not many companies have the foresight, the creativity, or the guts to put a living, breathing person on their Website, LinkedIn, or other social media.

Those that do use Video effectively will have a competitive advantage over their competition.

Whether your industry is highly commoditised or highly specialised, utilising custom videos on your LinkedIn profile and your Website will make you stand out.

- Do you have a clear call to action?

One of the issues we see is that a clear call to action is nowhere to be found on LinkedIn posts, blogs, social media, or websites.

If you are making your phone number a challenge to find (a pet hate of mine) or don't have a clear call to action or path that you want prospects to take, you will miss the boat when it comes to conversion.

A few simple changes will see a significant increase in your prospect conversions.

We would also suggest that you add your call to action on the Video on your site. You could even encourage clients to contact you within the Video.

- Strong Reputation.

Do you have a positive reputation and, if so, are you showcasing that on LinkedIn, other social media, and your Website?

We spend a lot of time helping our clients leverage their reputation to generate more prospects. We believe it is one of the most powerful conversion strategies to incorporate into your business today.

When somebody meets you in person, is referred to you, or sees one of your adverts — one of the first things most people do is "Google" your name as we all as your business name. They also use LinkedIn and read your story.

Some go so far as to look you up on Facebook. I have known clients lose a prospect because of their Facebook activity, so keep all your social media clean and tidy.

One prospective client was all clean-cut and uber professional on his LinkedIn; however, when we checked out his Facebook, his profile painted the picture of a drunken yob. Facebook was a more accurate reflection of the prospect's personality and lifestyle choices, and we chose not to take him on as a client.

By writing a book, your reputation will skyrocket.

If your prospects don't see positive reviews, a well-considered LinkedIn, social, and website presence, then your conversion will suffer.

- Do you have a USP (unique selling point)?

How do you set yourself apart from your competition?

Do you have a service guarantee or process that makes your business unique?

If so, highlight these differences and use them as conversion tools.

What can your prospects receive from you that they can't get with anybody else?

If you have used Video, the USPs will be so much easier to get over to your prospect.

Remember to promote your USPs within your video content.

- A 'freemium':

A 'freemium' is a simple way to encourage somebody through the door as a new customer if your business has a significant online presence.

Major 'freemium' providers are SKY, Netflix, Spotify, YouTube, ZOHO, Hubspot, and these companies have added $billions to their sales **per day** as a result. You can do the same.

We see this daily with companies offering free or low-cost access to their system, and you need to pay to upgrade to the version you will need. Some people stay on the free version however, most convert.

There is a psychological change that happens when somebody becomes a new customer that positions you to build trust, opens the door for future business, and taps into the thought-process of the lifetime value of a customer.

You will need to regularly communicate with these clients to encourage them to order more products or utilise your services more often.

- Track Conversion Rates:

Most businesses don't have any idea what their conversion rate is.

You can't improve something if you don't measure it.

How many website visitors are you turning into prospects (name, email, phone number)?

How many prospects are you turning into customers?

If you provide bids or quotes, how many proposals turn into new customers?

Use your CRM to track these numbers.

To Recap

Again, these are just a few ways that you can increase your conversion rate.

You will, of course, need to measure all of the above to be able to maximise every opportunity and gauge how your improvements are doing.

We believe that you should utilise your mentor and your coach to maximise your conversion rates. Don't forget to also keep your CRM consultants up to speed to enable them to hone your CRM to make your systems even more effective.

Exercise

Write down what you are going to do to increase conversion rates. You may wish to ask your coach to help you with this.

7. Increase Buying Frequency

How often does your typical customer buy from you?

Increasing the buying frequency is an essential aspect of growing your business and increasing your profits. Doubling your frequency doubles your turnover and is likely to quadruple your profits.

If you don't have a repeat custom business model, then work out to create repeat customers. Ideally, it would be best to create a subscription model where you put your clients on a monthly recurring payment, in the UK using Direct Debit and the rest of the World using services such as Stripe.

I took my 5 and 7-year-old daughters to a 'play place.' I noticed that the 50 plus adults were often without drinks on their tables. I met with the owner and suggested introducing table service because people don't like to get up and buy their drinks from the counter. People are lazy, especially when they are busy chatting! She made the changes, and drinks and food sales grew 400% immediately and increased the average spend per customer by 100%, and tripled the profits per person.

Keeping in regular contact with your customers is also likely to encourage them to buy more or visit you more. Interestingly, the soft play area I mentioned above doesn't take the details of their customers; whoops.

If they did, they could send out reminders, which will encourage their customers to visit more often. There are three similar units local to me and lots of alternatives. A text, email, or Facebook message is likely to increase the number of times we go.

You may wish to consult with your coach to assist you in increasing buying frequency. Here are a few of our suggestions:

- New Products or Services:

A new or revised product or service gives a further excuse to talk to your customer again, to engage with them, to invite them in to discuss if your new/ revised product or service is of value to them. You have already built up their trust, so you may wish to use that to your advantage.

Many of our clients introduce a new/ revised product or service every six months and ensure their clients and customers know about this.

McDonald's is good at bringing out new and revised products on various media and within stores. I'm a sucker for anything new and am always ordering the latest burger.

Apple is the World's best at this method. I'm a sucker for buying the latest iPhone!

We also suggest that you produce at least one new video of your new service and use this on LinkedIn, your website, and social media.

- Subscription or Membership Programs:

Turn part of your business into a subscription model? Your customers then pay you every month or annually instead of just one time or very sporadically.

Many of the World's most significant high-growth companies use this method. Just think of Sky, Netflix, Audible, YouTube, Spotify, Amazon, and even the gym you attend.

We have had many clients who have offered one-off services, and then we encouraged them to provide an annual review to their clients where the service was provided annually and paid for by Direct Debit.

One client turned a service selling for £4000 as a one-off into an £8000 annual fee with a minimum 5-year contract paid by Direct Debit. Just think about the increase in the lifetime value of that client.

The clients offered a report that analysed where his clients were obtaining their customers, the average costs of each, and where they believed they should focus their efforts.

Firstly, our client had massively underestimated the value of this service, a widespread issue. We conducted a simple exercise of calling his clients and asking them what they expected to pay for his service. Our first call was to a £15m company who had paid £4000 for the report. After a little prompting, the buyer admitted that she was expecting this level of report to cost close to £20,000. She was also expecting the supplier to be back in touch for an annual review, a situation that took our client by surprise.

Not only did he create repeat custom, but he also charged the clients the perceived value of his service and increased the average lifetime value of the client from £4,000 to £20,000.

Why did he price his service this way? He was thinking of his hourly rate rather than the value to the client. Stupid mistake? Yes, but a widespread one.

- Email Newsletter and messaging on LinkedIn and Facebook:

Many people think email is dead, which is far from the truth.

Keeping in front of your lead and customer via email regularly is a great way to maintain the relationship and stay top of mind.

Email and messaging are also great ways to communicate about special offers and increase buying frequency.

I have a favourite restaurant that we visited on a Tuesday. However, I noticed that he was always empty, save for one other table.

Eventually, I sat the owner down and asked him why it was empty, and he told me, "It has always been like this." I asked if he had the contact details of his clients? "No," was his answer.

We, first of all, asked him to gather his clients' contact details via a competition. Then he emailed all his customers with a special offer for a Tuesday. Now we don't have a quiet Tuesday night anymore; Tuesday is one of his busiest nights!

Emailing and messaging your prospects that did not buy is also important.

We email and message all our old prospects going back up to 5 years every 90 days. Every email we send out, old prospects engage with us, and each client we convert costs pennies.

Be careful to ensure that you adhere to your national Data Protection and Emailing laws.

Remember that some of your prospects may not have bought from you due to timing. Keep in touch, and when the timing is right for them, then you should be front of mind.

Exercise

List the methods you are going to use to increase buyer frequency. You may wish to include your coach in this exercise

8. Increase the Average Transaction Amount

If your average transaction is £100, how can you increase that to £110 or £125?

If you offer a high-value service at £4000, how can you increase this to £8000 or even £80,000?

To calculate your average transaction amount, add up all of your transactions and divide by the total number of transactions.

For example, if you had a total of £1m in revenue and you had 1000 total transactions, then your average transaction amount would be £1000.

Increasing your average transaction amount will make a considerable difference to your bottom line, even if it is small percentage-wise. Here are some potential ways to improve your average transaction amount.

- Up-sell & Cross-sell:

How often have you purchased something on impulse that you weren't necessarily planning on buying? I know I have, and I will continue to do.

McDonald's is famous for the ultimate upsell — "Do you want fries with that"? Around 30% of customers say yes to that question who would not have ordered fries.

What opportunities might exist in your business to offer an upsell to an existing customer? You may wish to have a quick brain storm with your team and maybe your coach to come up with some ideas.

For example, if you're a firm of Solicitors, how many clients do you ask about their will? Around 1 in 2 won't have one that is fit for purpose.

Has your client a mum and dad in need of a will? Have they a Power of Attorney in place for themselves and their parents? When will your client move home next? The list goes on.

What if you are supplying a conservatory? Indeed you then have an opportunity to sell conservatory blinds? Heating systems? Air conditioning? Windows for the rest of the house? Referral to a kitchen company? Referral to a painter and decorator?

- Follow up Promotions:

If you sell anything online, you could also include a special offer on a thank you page or follow-up email. A client who has bought from you once is likely to buy from you again. Amazon is amazing at this. I receive emails every week offering me what they suggest I would love to buy. They make £thousands every year from me alone with this method.

An often-used Internet and social media marketing strategy is multiple upsells, allowing the purchaser to purchase several additional items. This can be conducted straight after the original purchase or regularly.

For example, you might have a small temptation offer at £299, with an upsell offer of £2,299, and another upsell offer of £4,999 — all on thank you pages, follow-up emails, or LinkedIn/Facebook messages.

- Increase your prices:

Small business owners are hesitant to raise prices, which is often a contributory factor as to why they stay small.

Competition is real, and the threat of losing customers based on price will happen. However, in many businesses, you may be able to raise your prices without any issues.

We have helped clients double their prices, and more clients have bought from them!

We were one of them.

Keep in mind that most purchases are not based on price.

We have witnessed many situations where the business owner is afraid to raise prices, but they need to build a sustainable business model.

Have you also considered the value of your product or service from your client's point of view?

Have you been selling your services based on their cost to you rather than the value to the client?

We always ask a client about their prices. They often tell us what the cost to them is, and then they add 30%. Where is the client in this thought process? Are they considering the value the client feels they are receiving? No.

So what is the value of your service to your customer? Have you ever asked?

For example, one client was selling a high-end report on company sales performance for £4000 as a one-off event. With a bit of coaxing, they increased this to £8000 with an annual review each year with an expected client lifetime of 5 years. The following client they met, when asked how much the client thought the report was worth, they stated £18,000. Have a guess what happened to their new pricing policy and their profits!

We had another client who had been in business for 30 years, with many customers being on his books for over ten years. We asked him about his prices, and the client was convinced that he was on a par with his competition.

The reality was very different.

After conducting a day's worth of research, we found that he was underpricing by 30%. We turned the business from a $1.7m turnover to $2.3m within weeks. His profits went from $80k to $550k without spending any money.

Remember the Russian Serviced Accommodation client of ours I mentioned earlier? He charged 'market rate' until we asked him to double the rate. His occupancy increased, and profits tripled.

We often suggest that clients should conduct professional research to ascertain what their pricing should be.

- Tiered pricing:

Your services can be offered at different levels to suit different customers.

Not everyone wants your full service, so consider having several options for your customers, e.g., a bronze, silver, and gold service, and let the customer pick the level they want.

We do this within all our offerings. For example, our managed LinkedIn service starts at £199 pm, and there are several other options all the way to £5,000 pm. We have an offer for their budgets and the demands of their business. If we have a freelancing business coach who wants a client every few months, they will pick the £199 version. On the other hand, a larger company wanting a considerable volume and has the infrastructure to handle the work will choose a higher level of service.

Could you always upsell to a higher level of service at a later date?

Not only is it likely that more people will buy if the gold service is a higher value, but you may also have increased your average sale value.

We suggest that you conducted market research to ascertain the levels of service different clients would like.

You could also involve your coach to help you with this.

- Upgrade your Target Audience:

If your business were selling 1000 items at £1000 profit each, would you consider selling just 200 much better quality products at £10,000 profit each?

This is not a rhetorical question, even though the second option doubles profits from £1m to £2m.

Selling much higher value products or services could demand a fundamental and significant pivot from your current model. It takes nerve and money to shift like this; however, the benefits could be huge!

We recently met a web designer and wanted to shift from producing low-grade WordPress websites with an average price of £1000 to a web designer focused on creating much more sophisticated SaaS sites with an average value of £20,000.

The client had to cut down his staff from 40 to 10, move office, and only focus on larger clients. A no-brainer? However, he had no choice; however, he required over £250,000 to finance this quantum shift in his business model.

These methods take guts and determination to implement, and you may wish to work with your coach. You may also benefit from running this by a Mastermind Group that you are a member of or your coach/ mentor.

Exercise

Write down what you can do to increase the Average Transaction Amount.

9. Increase Your Profit Margin.

Ahh, profit. That [minor] detail that so many business owners forget about so quickly.

As business owners and entrepreneurs, our number one priority should be to turn a profit. You cannot serve your customers without turning a profit.

Why? Because to stay in business long term and be able to fuel your "why," … we have to be profitable.

Here are a couple of ways that you may wish to focus on to improve your margins.

- Systemise everything:

If you've owned franchise business models, you know that they have documented their business process and become a system-based and not people-based business.

We have much detail within this book on systemising. Why? Because the more your systems are documented, the more you can train your team to consistently produce the same product efficiently and effectively, therefore reducing your costs and increasing your average profit margin.

To systemise, you will need CRM because CRM will underpin all your systems and enable you to run a global company from your laptop.

Remember, CRM is no longer a luxury. It's a necessity!

- Marketing and Technical Automation:

We are working on ourselves and believe it provides a significant opportunity to help you benefit from automation.

Last year we moved to marketing automation software to help automate the redundant, repetitive tasks that otherwise take human capital to accomplish. Even in a modest business, this can create from £20,000 to £100,000 in extra profit.

It has been a great move, and, quite frankly, we've only scratched the surface.

During any given week, we have hundreds of small, automated tasks working in the background, on our behalf, that we never have to touch.

This might include an email, a text, a whatsapp message, a phone call, or assigning a task to one of our team.

By automating, you can accomplish so much more, freeing up your time to do other higher-level activities and increasing your average profit margin.

You will need CRM to be able to do this, of course!

- CRM.

CRM is short for Customer Relationship Management. CRM is a 'must have' for all businesses of any size. Gone are the days where CRM was a luxury.

If your competitor has CRM and you do not, they will have a serious advantage over you, and you may find it difficult to compete.

CRM should underpin your sales, operational, and accounting process and underpin the automation of your business systems.

For example, if a funding client comes via Facebook in my office, they are sent a link to book a call and read some info. Once they book a call, each step is then automated from this point on. This saves around 2 man-hours per client.

With a CRM, you can see the whole pipeline; you can see what all your employees are doing or not doing.

You will be able to systemise most of your processes, even taking most mundane tasks and automating them, saving you time, money and reducing human error.

With a CRM, you make life easier for yourself, reduce your costs and dramatically increase your profits.

If you want to scale and eventually sell your business, then **you must have a CRM.**

There are many CRM's, and you should research your ideal fit for your business now and in the future.

Implementing CRM should not be undertaken on your own; you will mess it all up: We did. We strongly suggest that you use an expert to build the system with you. This will save you time and money on many levels.

To Recap.

Increasing your profit margins per client is an ongoing battle, and we would suggest that you engage a suitably qualified coach or mentor.

A coach or mentor will help you drive down the costs per client while ensuring that your standards are as high as required. You may also need the services of a suitably qualified Finance Director to support your team.

Exercise

Write down what you are going to do to Increase your Profit Margin. You may need your coach or mentor to support you with this exercise.

10. Increase the lifespan of your client.

What if you could keep clients for 10, 20, or even 30 years? I have quite a few businesses that I still buy from after 10, 20, and even 30 years, so why not think about how you can generate such long-term loyalty. iTunes, Sky, my Gym, utility provider, House insurance, Virgin airlines, and I could probably add another 10 to this list.

Just think about the fantastic relationship you would have with the client? Just think how many referrals a loyal client will refer to you over 30 years.

Is it possible to retain a client for 30 years or more? The simple answer is yes.

We believe that it is, for some businesses; however, regardless of the business you are in, you will need to have gained 'trusted advisor' status with the client.

- Earn 'Trusted advisor' Status.

What does it take to earn Trusted Advisor status with your clients and customers?

Research by CSO Insights, the Aberdeen Group, and others have shown that just telling your sales team to be trusted advisors has not worked:

Win rates have fallen considerably over the last two decades. Client behaviours seem to be saying that they don't trust salespeople's intent and don't see them as a credible advisor.

Let's explore three fundamental principles that point to becoming a trusted advisor.

11. Creating the Trust in a Trusted Advisor.

Great sales professionals will say trust is the foundation of relationship selling. Great salespeople understand that if you don't have a strong, trusting relationship with your client, you will never be viewed as a trusted advisor, and you will reduce your success levels. We concur.

Firstly, creating a trusting relationship requires both a mindset and a set of actions. As a mindset, a salesperson must genuinely believe that their job is to help the customer or client solve their problem.

We believe that a salesperson that mentally calculates their commission during a sale will probably lose the sale—That's because many clients can see that the salesman is more interested in making the sale than they are in the client's needs and expectations.

"The best' sales process does not 'sell'; it enables the customer to buy."

In addition to having the right mindset, trusted advisors demonstrate their interest in helping customers. The most extraordinary discipline of relationship selling is knowing how to show empathy, establish credibility and competence, and anticipate customers' concerns.

This mindset and set of actions that your business must have to approach the sales process with authenticity, passion, and positive intent must be created. Relationship selling focuses on who you are and what you do and is communicated by actions focused on your clients and their needs. This leads to trust.

12. Facilitate Your Customer's Buying Process

For many years sales leaders have taught salespeople that they must follow a systematic sales process.

Considerable resources have gone into developing procedures, software, websites, and checklists—almost demanding that there is only one way to structure the "sale." We believe that this is wrong.

The best "selling process" does not sell; it enables the client to buy.

The antithesis of the trusted advisor is the salesperson, who believes that if they follow a well defined sales process, they will be successful.

The action of a trusted advisor is to help the customer buy the way they want to buy, **not** how you want to sell.

Think of a Doctor? When you visit them with an ailment, do they start selling their favourite drug? No, they ask questions to ascertain the problem, and then they work out what the best course of action is, based on their knowledge.

Is your Doctor a trusted advisor to you because of this method?

We believe that the discipline required to facilitate the clients buying process is:

1. Helping the client discover the urgency behind their need

2. Helping the client to define the problem that needs to be solved.

3. Helping the client see what elements of a solution have value for them and which parts don't.

4. Helping the client gather support for the answer within their organisation, creating alignment for action.

5. Help the client to see why they should buy your service rather than anything else where they could spend their money on.

Helping a client to buy cannot be done by following a seller-focused sales process. It requires a two-way conversation between you, the trusted advisor, and the client to understand the problem and recognise the urgency to solve the problem.

13. Making Sense of Complexity

Clients today have almost an infinite amount of information available at their fingertips. Too much information.

Your responsibility as their trusted advisor is to help your client to bring clarity to the complexity. To cut through the noise in the market to find the right solution that will solve your client's problem.

As the trusted advisor, your discipline is to link the solution to the advantages and benefits for the customer.

As the trusted advisor, you must listen to the client and share business insights, clarify to ensure understanding, reduce confusion, and present possible solutions to the problem that satisfies and delights the customer.

To Recap; Applying Actionable Discipline To Achieve Trusted Advisor Status

Actionable discipline, however, is going beyond just what is necessary and taking the time to do what they know what you should do. This takes a fantastic Mindset, accountability, and leadership to achieve.

While all salespeople take action, most take the path of least resistance, doing what is most accessible or what they think is necessary to make a sale.

However, it takes discipline to become a trusted advisor. Once you earn trusted advisor status, it is a coveted position that provides greater business-level value to your clients and your organisation.

It would be best if you took ownership of creating trust with your clients.

Focusing on becoming the Trusted will produce ongoing, long-term relationships that present multiple opportunities to sell and service your clients while enabling your clients to buy how they want to buy.

Exercise

Write down what you are going to do to increase the lifespan of your client. You may wish to involve the coach in this process.

24. Grow More Rapidly by Buying Businesses.

———————✦———————

By far, the fastest, lowest cost, and lowest risk method to grow your business and wealth is to buy another business.

I truly believe that this is by far the best way to grow your business. Sure, you need to action the rest of this book, its just that buying businesses will turbo your growth beyond your wildest dreams.

I'm still kicking myself that I did not realise this much earlier.

Why have I waited until 50% through this book to drop this bombshell?

You need to control your mindset and understand the mechanics of growing a business before you should buy another one.

A trainer called Jonathan Jay teaches people to buy businesses, and i believe that his philosophy is seriously flawed because he states that anyone can buy a business and make it a success. That's true on the surface, but if you don't have. a growth mindset and don't know how to think like an investor, you will fail.

Why do I think buying businesses is such a great strategy? Let's say you are already at £1m in turnover, and it's taken you five years of hard slog to reach this level. By buying a business, you could add a further

£1m+ to this turnover simply by purchasing another business that ideally compliments yours.

For example, if you have a dental practice, how many other dentists are potentially for sale within 30mins drive? 30? 50? Whatever the number, with focus, you could buy a further 10- 15 other dentists over two years. If each of these has a turnover of £1m, your 'Group' would now be turning over £10m-£15m. Sounds interesting, now doesn't it.

If the average pre-tax profit is 40%, you go from £400K to £4m-£8m within two years.

Once you own a group you can either hold onto the business, or you can sell it. To sell a £5m pa profit business to private equity is likely to produce a cheque of £30m. £30m because you decided to buy a few businesses as your primary growth strategy? Sounds good to me.

It gets better.

When you buy these businesses, you can centralise many of the operational, marketing, and accounting systems, rapidly increasing the profits from each of these new acquisitions.

It gets even better....

Smaller businesses have a lower value when sold than larger ones. A small business with a turnover of £500k and profit of £100k is only really worth a maximum of £200k to £300k. And that only if it meets a large list of requirements that very few will meet.

If you buy 10 of these businesses, the value is not £2m-£3m, the value is likely to be more like £600k each or £6m in total.

When you have purchased several companies and then unified the systems, Private Equity businesses are then very interested in buying your business. Hence, the multiple of profit goes from x2 to x6.

Six times multiply on £6m pa is a £36m payday. That's going to change your life and the life of generations to come.

Once you have built one group you can do it again and again.

What type of businesses should you buy?

Ideally, it would be best to buy businesses where you have at least an understanding of it. That's not a hard and fast rule; however, for the first year of buying businesses, this may be the most effective strategy.

The business could be

1. A direct competitor.
2. A business in the same space as you selling the same service but not a competitor.
3. A business in your sector but working with a niche
4. A business that supplies services to you and others
5. A business that sells services to the same clients as you serve.

Once you become experienced, you may choose to buy a series of businesses in a sector you don't understand. You would need to build a team with plenty of experience in that sector.

Buying a business without risking your own cash

I had this all wrong. I truly believed that you needed to borrow oodles of your cash to buy another business, and this delusion held me back for years.

I have and will continue to buy businesses for as little as £1. You would be surprised at how successful a business can be that still sells for just £1.

I've even been given a £million turnover business for nothing.

You can finance the assets of the business you are buying to pay the owner for the shares for those you need to buy.

You can pay the owner over an agreed period of time. This is the most common arrangement. I typically pay over a deferred period of 3 years.

What you need to avoid is buying a business with your hard-earned money and paying the seller upfront.

No matter how much due diligence you do, no matter how many warranties they sign, if you pay upfront, you are at risk.

If the business is viable and doing well, the owner will likely accept being paid monthly over 2-5 years. They are then free to do what they want to know while you help the management team to build the business.

Once you have ownership, you will need to make sure that you improve the business ability to pay the old owners and draw a good profit yourself

If things go wrong and it transpires the seller was lying about their business, you can reduce the amount you pay them.

With some companies, you may need to pay them some money upfront. You could do this many ways, and one of the smarter ways is to refinance some of the assets in their business to pay them the funds they need upfront.

If the business is 'distressed' or the seller needs to move quickly, you could end up buying it for £1. These are my favourite deals but you should avoid this type of business unless you are experienced in fixing broken companies.

On occasions, £1 is all you will pay, and on others you may need to pay the seller over a matter of years. Either way, you can avoid doing some of the due diligence typically required because you risk less of your money.

Why will someone sell to you?

There are many reasons why someone wants to sell.

Examples

- They wish to retire
- They are ill, and they need to focus on their health
- Their spouse is sick and then need to focus more time on supporting them
- They are tired of running the business
- They have taken the business as far as they can.
- They wish to focus on another business they have
- They have financial issues
- They have relationship issues
- They are emigrating
- The business is losing money, and they don't want to keep bailing it out.

People will sell their business for many reasons, and you need to uncover their reason at the outset of your conversation with them.

Contrary to popular belief, with many sellers, the highest priority is not money. If the seller is retiring, their priority may be that their legacy is continued. It may be that they want to secure the future of their employees, who have been loyal to them for decades. I like this type of seller because their heart is in the right place.

For others, speed may be their priority. Uncovering their reasons for selling is paramount because your entire deal will be based on it.

How to source deals.

I believe that the ideal business to buy is not one currently for sale.

Businesses that are already for sale are likely to have an exaggerated value of the business put into their heads by a 'business broker.'

Business brokers are often only in business to take a 'marketing fee' from a seller, and as such, they tend to exaggerate the value of the business massively.

Brokers cause you several issues, and there are so many businesses wishing to sell to you, you may as well walk away from most businesses that are for sale with a broker.

Have a meeting with them. Just expect these deals to take longer and be quite challenging.

The best way to source deals is to understand whom you wish to target and then acquire the data.

Once you have the data, construct a letter and then write to the owner. Yes, write, not email, Facebook, or Linkedin messages. Write.

People love receiving letters these days, and one that uses a quality envelope and quality letterhead will go down well.

To obtain one company to buy you may need to write 500 letters. If you want to buy ten businesses, that may require 10,000 letters. The cost of this is insignificant. Just make sure that you are not stuffing the envelopes!

You can also

- Post on Facebook Groups that you are a buyer.

- Send messages directly to members of these groups

- Post on Linkedin that you are a buyer of businesses

- Build a database on LinkedIn of the connections you are interested in

- Send messages to your relevant connections on Linkedin.

- Advertise in magazines that sell to your target audience.

Keep in mind that you should delegate much of the above, and you need to focus on the high-value activity of actually talking to the seller.

Creating volume deal flow

If you wish to buy five businesses over the next 12 months, you may need to speak with a hundred. To speak with a hundred owners you may need to write to five thousand.

So buying a business is no different from prospecting for a client. You will need to use your CRM to track your deal flow. You will need to create a strategy to handle the deal flow.

Ideally, you should always have several conversations going all at once. This way, you will not be emotionally attached to any of the deals, so you can walk away if the deal does not stack.

Being able to walk away is a powerful tool, and the seller needs to know that you have lots of other deals on the table. This will ensure that you don't buy businesses you should walk away from or pay too much for one.

Meeting with the seller of the business.

Doing the deal

A golden rule when buying a business is NOT to make an offer.

So you have found out why someone is selling, now is the time to ask the seller what they want for their business.

Don't ever, and I mean never make an offer and if the seller doesn't tell you what they are looking for, then walk away from the deal.

If they are serious, most will come back to you. Cap in hand.

Putting the onus on them to tell you how much they are looking for is likely to result in a considerably lower figure than you are thinking. Conversely, their valuation and financial requirements will be crazy high.

Once they have told you the price, then you can go from there.

The first step is to sign an NDA that means that during the next 8 weeks they cannot sell to anyone else. It also means that you won't discuss anything with anyone except your team.

Sellers are typically nervous that the information they share with you should be confidential.

You should always use your NDA and make sure it's one written by your Solicitors.

Ensure that the seller is aware that you have lots of deals going and always stay uber professional. Don't let your ego or emotions play any part in the deal.

Ensure the seller knows that you can walk away easily, which gives you huge leverage levels when negotiating.

Your business buying team

It would be best if you did not attempt to buy a business on your own. You need a professional team.

- M&A Solicitor/ Lawyer/ Advocate

A Mergers and Acquisitions solicitor/ Lawyer is a critical member of your team because, without them, you cannot construct a deal properly, and this is likely to lead to a financial disaster or two.

- Accountant

Your accountant needs to be familiar with M&A, group structures, and ideally, your target business type.

- Due diligence expert

A due diligence expert will undertake all the required checks of all businesses beyond the heads of terms stage. They will then compile you a report on the business, warts, and all. This report may lead you to walk away on occasions and enable you to negotiate the best possible deal for you.

- Fractional FD

An experienced FD will uncover all the financials and both the weaknesses and strengths of the business. Once you have bought the business, you may well bring them back in the remodel the business to maximise its profits

- Fractionals SD

Most businesses have ineffective sales and marketing plans and strategies, and a fractional FD can uncover the weaknesses and the strengths of the business. Once the business is purchased, they can then come in to fix many of the issues.

- Fractional HR

With most of the businesses you buy, you will be taking on staff. You will need an HR expert because you may need to make some people redundant, amend employment contracts, etc.

Fix the business you buy

All businesses you buy will need fixing. This could be pretty minor; however, the fixing required is likely to be extensive.

You may need to make several people redundant; you may need to employ some more people.

You may need to arrange alternative funding and make sure you use a reputable broker.

The current bank may need to be changed, and if there is outstanding funding, you should meet with the relationship manager straight away.

Most businesses have an inefficient sales process and strategy, and you will need to fix the holes in the new business.

Most businesses also have their pricing wrong, and repricing the service should be undertaken with great care.

Many of the aspects that need fixing will bring in significant increases in profits. On the other hand, some will cost you cash in the short term.

Fixing a business is much easier than creating a business.

The Action Plan

You will need to create an action plan for dealing with the new businesses for the first 90 days.

You may need to make people redundant, move the office, take out complete departments and then transfer these tasks to your primary business. Whatever needs to happen needs to be planned for.

The planning for this is essential, and once you have a winning formula, you can rinse and repeat many times over

Your Mentor

Your mentor will be critical in ensuring that you make a success of buying businesses. Buying a business is not something we would recommend without support. To find out more about how we can help you, please visit our website www.thegrowthgurus.co.uk/mentor

Our plans

We plan on buying 20 businesses per year and selling on 'groups' of businesses into the PE market, ideally every 2 to 3 years maximum.

Most business owners have one sale event in their lifetimes; I have had a few already and plan on having another ten at a minimum value of £10m each.

To Recap

The fastest way to grow your business is to buy other businesses. Period. I wish I had known this and saved me a massive amount of work!

Exercise

Identify the types of businesses you would like to buy, and then get in touch with me to chat about how we can help you make this a reality

25. Build Your Dream Team

W e have yet to meet a business owner or entrepreneur who has built a highly profitable business and achieved great wealth without a fantastic team working with them.

If you don't have a team, you're either a freelancer or just' self-employed'; *period.*

With social media, it may appear that someone is a one-person success story, but I can assure you that this will not be the case. They will have a whole team behind them.

Building your team is, by far, one of the most important aspects of growing a truly successful business. You need a team to develop your current business, and you need a team to build all the other businesses you buy.

Getting this part wrong can bring a swift end to your enterprise or, at best, seriously reduce your profits.

We have touched upon the subject throughout this book, and this section dedicates itself to helping with the knotty dilemmas and challenges that you will face.

If the time has come to admit that you can't do it all, this chapter may help you figure out just who you need on your dream team, where to find them, and how to hire them.

In the early days of setting up your own business, it's natural to try to do as much as possible yourself.

It may feel like the most cost-effective, comfortable, sensible way to do things initially, or so you believe it to be.

The reality is, doing everything yourself slows down your growth, drives your profits down, drives your customers away, and will lead you to an eventual failure of your business.

As your venture starts to trade and client volumes increase, you will find yourself stretched thinner and thinner with an increasing number of hours spent in the business. Eventually, you'll find you can't continue to oversee operations, sales, accounting, delivery, and marketing--and hope to continue to grow your business. If you do, your business is likely to stall, falter, and then fail.

Before you reach this point, it's time to start bringing other high-level managers on board to help you realise your dreams and ambitions.

It would be best if you built a dream team that can manage all the critical areas of your business to take it to maximise its performance.

Building your dream team demands matching jobs to people's strengths (covered earlier). That means giving people responsibilities according to their skill level, not based on how close a friend they are or if they are related to you or whether you just like their can-do personality.

That includes you as well--please don't be a dick and give yourself an impressive title and job unless you're suitable for the job.

The fact is, the majority of intelligent business owners and entrepreneurs hire their own 'boss' when they realise their skills are better utilised elsewhere in the company. I did this twice, and once I had resigned from my role as MD, our growth was awe-inspiring! I ended up taking more and more holidays because every time I went away, our business improved!

The primary step of handing over control is not easy for the ego to take unless you have been working on your Mindset and you are more focused on delivering an excellent service to your clients.

This was when I realised I was not the ideal 'operator' of a business, and I was the quintessential 'investor.' I just had to get out of my own way.

If you have one of those so-called 'family businesses,' you need to take extra special note of the last few lines.

The bottom line is this;

If you employ your relatives. in jobs that they are not suitable for, it will cripple your business performance, your business growth will falter, and the business will eventually fail.

Very few 'family businesses' succeed at a level they could have reached because they tend to focus on the wrong thing when bringing in a management team. **Family is very seldom best.**

I have heard arguments on the lines of 'At least I can trust my family. However, this is often naïve, and now that you have read this far into this book, I am sure you will understand why?

When it is appropriate to hire a management team, you'll need to find people to fill the following roles:

The following explanations cover the basics of each of the management team roles.

- Chief Empowerment Officer (CEO).
  And this is not always going to be the founder!

Most people use 'Chief Executive Officer'; however, there are x100 times more 'ceos' with one employee than real ones. Secondly, the word 'executive' is at best pompous.

The CEO has overall responsibility for:

- Accountable for the vision of the business,
- Oversight of the management team and key people in the business to ensure that they are the right 'fit.'
- Maintaining and enhancing the brand in the market.
- Being the Thought Leader for the business.
- Continually researching and connecting with the key players in your market.
- Reporting to the rest of the Board and Chairman (if you have one)
- Looking out to buy more businesses.
- Preparing the business for sale and founders for an exit.

The CEO determines the company's overall values and strategy. They hire, build, motivate and replace the senior management team. The CEO makes the final call on how resources such as cash are distributed.

The CEO's skills must include vision, strategic thinking, the ability to rise above the daily grind and decide where their sector and business are headed. They must then be able to determine the business's ideal route for navigating the future market conditions. They have to be able to take calculated risks.

They have a solid entrepreneurial bias already and have a robust Growth Mindset.

The CEO's essential skill, however, is in hiring and managing the management team. An excellent management team can cover a CEO's shortcomings (especially if the CEO is also the founder).

A CEO may be able to create the strategy, predict the future of the market and the sector and control the budget. However, if they don't hire the right management team, they have to master it all themselves, leading to stagnation and eventual business failure. So the CEO needs to identify and hire the best and fire those who don't work out.

If the founder acts as the CEO, you may need to consider a professional CEO before becoming mired in the details for way too long and can't pull yourself out. After all, as the founder, you do not want to be giving yourself a role that you neither like nor feel comfortable in, especially if your continued tenure damages profits. Your profits!

CEOs think about where the organisation is going, the people and processes needed to get there, and how they'll work in the current market. If you like details rather than strategy, hire a CEO to do the job for you. If you are restless and want to 'move on to the next big idea,' then move on and hire a great CEO.

The alternative is stagnation and eventual failure.

If you cannot afford a full-time CEO, then you could consider two options:

1. Find a superstar CEO who will buy into your company and come on board for sweat equity *1 or

2. You could hire a fractional professional CEO until you can afford to pay for a full-time professional.

*1 What does 'Sweat equity' actually mean? Regarding an early-stage business, sweat equity means exchanging a high salary for shares in your company. You will need to ensure that you garner professional help when distributing shares in this way. You will need to ensure that you have shareholders' agreements in place and that you give the correct form of shares away. You will also need to create a robust share transfer strategy to ensure that your new-found partner is incentivised correctly and what you can do if your new exec fails to perform. Please don't venture into this arena without the support, and a good quality coach should be fully aware of how to support you to handle this delicate area without catching a cold.

- Operations Director

An OD handles a company's complex operational details. The company's OD ensures the business can deliver day after day. He calculates what needs to be measured so he can tell if things are going well.

He and his team create the system to manage the business, track the measurements, and constantly improve performance.

Naturally, the OD will be leading the implementation and continual improvement of the CRM. After all, the CRM will make the ODs' job so much easier.

Within a single-location retail business, the store manager is effectively the OD. However, they are a hands-on, sleeves-rolled-up type of OD. When you expand to multiple units or require your business to be fully systemised, it's time to hire an OD who revels in measurements, operations, and details.

If you cannot afford a full-time OD, then you could consider two other options:

1. Find a superstar OD who will buy into your company and come on board for sweat equity or

2. You could hire a fractional professional OD for the price of a junior member of your staff.

- Finance Director.

Your FD handles the financial matters. They also create budgets, financing strategies, financial projections, and planning, working closely with the CEO and OD. The FD builds the control systems that monitor your company's financial health and predict its economic future. The FD is the "bad guy" who won't let you buy that cool video conferencing equipment and makes you focus resources on generating more fee-paying clients.

The FD will be busy figuring out which customers, business lines, and products are profitable so that you can pay yourself even more of a dividend next year.

You'll know when you need an FD, and we will give you a clue; as soon as is feasibly possible.

Unless you lie awake at night dreaming about numbers, you need to bring someone on board who does, and that is **not a bookkeeper;** it's a fully qualified CFO. A fully qualified and experienced CFO will pay for themselves within just a couple of months.

Let me get one vital point out straight away. Your accountant **is not** an FD, and you should not treat him like one. Accountants are excellent at looking at your business through the rearview mirror. What do we mean by this? They are great at assessing your performance to date and, to a modest degree analysing the issues.

That is what they are trained to do. An FD, on the other hand, like any good driver, checks the mirrors; however, his focus is on the road ahead. This takes a level of vision and imagination that most statutory accountants lack.

So please don't ever make the foolhardy mistake of asking your accountant to advise you on growth; it will often end in tears. They simply don't have the necessary Mindset and imagination hence why they spend their lives counting other people's money!

Money is your business's blood, and in business, cash flow is vital. Don't you know the difference between cash flow and profit? Run-- don't walk--to the nearest phone and find yourself an FD.

If you cannot afford a full-time FD, then you could consider two options:

1. Find a superstar FD who will buy into your company and come on board for sweat equity.

2. There are several companies operating panels of FD's who can support you part-time. a Fractional FD can cost you as little as a part-time junior member of staff...

An FD is typically a qualified Management Accountant **and not** a Chartered Accountant (CA). A CA may be great as a Financial Controller but not a CFO.

This is a crucial point!

• Marketing or Sales Director. (MSD)

We believe the MSD should be your first hire after your PA. The reason is simple: build your sales first because this produces cash. The

MSD owns the marketing strategy, and this includes the sales strategy.

The MSD will

- Lean and mentor the marketing and sales team.
- Learn your industry, sector, or profession inside out
- Help you position your product,
- Differentiate your business from your competitors' products,
- Create your sales channels,
- Recruit distributors,
- Recruit referrers,
- Work with social media, LinkedIn and Search Engine Optimisation, Pay Per Click, and Social Media Agencies and make sure customers learn to crave your product or service.

A business's success depends mainly on marketing and sales. Therefore you need an MFD. That might be the founder, but only if the founder has time to keep up with your competitors, oversee the marketing implementation, and still do the rest of your tasks and do it to a world-class level. Otherwise, you need an MFD.

If you cannot afford a full-time MFD, then you could consider two options:

1. Find a superstar MFD who will buy into your company and come on board for sweat equity,

2. Take on a fractional MFD who will be able to start the process of formalising your strategies, your marketing, and sales systems and implement these. All for the cost of a junior member of your team.

- IT Director.

An ITD should keep up with trends in technology, integrate those trends into the company's strategy and make sure the company keeps its technology current. However, they should not be buying new toys and leading-edge technology just because it's the latest, greatest thing out there.

Unless you're in SaaS or some other tech-heavy sector, we would suggest outsourcing this role and building up your management in other areas first.

- HR Director.

The role of HRD in a growing company is critical and is often an afterthought in many businesses in the UK and the US. The HRD should make fundamental contributions to the organisation's culture, development, and staffing..

I didn't realise the importance of an HRD for years, which held back our growth and cost me £millions.

The HRD develops systems and processes that hire employees, retaining employees, and deal with all aspects of talent within your business.

The HRD ensures that these employees are also congruent with your company's culture. This is no easy task! You don't just need bums on seats; you need the right bums on seats, or your teams' values will not be aligned with yours.

The role of the HRD must run parallel to the needs of your developing and growing business. Your increasingly successful business should start to become more adaptable, resilient, quick to change direction to follow your client needs. An excellent HRD needs to recognise that your competitors will vie for talent in the coming years, and you need to be able to recruit and retain the best of the best.

At the same time, your HRD will have responsibility for day-to-day employee issues, benefits administration, payroll, and employee paperwork.

Alongside you, the founder, the HRD is heavily involved in defining and developing your culture, which will play a critical role in the success of your business.

Taking on a full-time HRD is typically far too expensive for most sub £1m businesses; however, plenty of highly experienced directors are willing to work on a fractional basis until you need someone full-time.

- Finding Your Team Members

Unfortunately, great Directors don't grow on trees (and you wouldn't want to hire the ones that do). Since their decisions and values are likely to make or break your business: **you need the best**.

If you have the funds available (a perfect reason to raise investment capital), executive search firms are an excellent choice. Although they do charge high fees to find candidates, they should conduct the necessary due diligence and only offer you with screened candidates, so they can be a time and energy-saver. They also monitor the market for talent and can likely reach candidates you couldn't approach on your own.

Search firms often specialise in sector, function, geography, and job level, so if you decide to hire one, make sure they focus on your areas of interest.

Networking is an excellent way to find your Directors. Let your networks know what kind of people you are looking for, including

LinkedIn. Then get one-on-one introductions and take your candidates to lunch to test the chemistry.

Inlinked our preferred Linkedin agency can do a superb job of recruiting your dream team. www.inlinked.co.uk

Keep in mind that there is plenty of evidence that shows us that while chemistry is essential, being likable is not a precursor for success. Your new executive Board needs to perform, and being likable is unlikely to be your highest need for this outcome.

Once you've found a potential candidate, how will you know for sure they can do the job?

Executives have a considerable impact on your employees, customers, systems, and profits, so it's vital to check them out thoroughly.

Cleaver people create cleaver bullshit.

Call each and all of their references and listen between the lines to what they are telling you. Listen out for less-than-glowing opinions.

Remember that you can always consider a sweat equity position for all of your team.

- Interviewing Tips

When it comes time to meet with your potential candidate, there are a few things to know that will make your task easier:

- **Make sure your candidate knows the job.** If your Marketing and Sales Director-to-be doesn't know the difference between marketing and sales, then it's time they left the room.

- **Interview for chemistry.** Do you trust the candidate? Do you want to spend time with them?

You don't want a team member you don't get on with, no matter how talented they may be. I once went skiing with a prospective Director; it didn't go well, so that was the end.

- **Talk to people from the candidate's former employer.** Are their claims of brilliance reflected in what their former peers and team have to say? Find out how they contributed to the company's culture, how they got on with others.

In your small business, cultural issues can be every bit as important as getting things done. Remember: Culture eats strategy for breakfast.

- **Always hire the most brilliant people you can.** Here's an excellent guide to follow: Every new hire should increase your company's average IQ. This means **they should all be much more intelligent than you**. Get used to it, relish it. (That's not a high bar for me to reach!)

- **Look for evidence of learning ability.** Will your new team member repeat mistakes they have made in the past, or will they learn from those errors and adapt that knowledge to benefit your growing business?

- **Use "behaviour description interviewing" techniques.** Don't ask about their principles, knowledge, or "what if" stories. Instead, ask your potential dream team member to share specific past events and what they did about them. Their stories will reveal their abilities, skills, values. For example, you might ask an FD to describe a budget they created and how they handled it when a department exceeded their budget and asked for more.

Warning: ***Be very, very wary of hiring friends or family members***. They may expect you to trust them and just assume they have a high skill level.

What's worse, you may assume they have a high skill level without any evidence to the contrary. Unless you are very clear about the boundaries between friendship and work, you may find your friendship in ruins over workplace disagreements

- Making The Deal

Once you've found the dream team member you'd like to hire, you have to entice them to join your team. There are no standard rules for the optimum deal to offer them. Low-grade workers may be thrilled to get cash, but senior people are not so easily satisfied.

They often want shares, more pay, and a bonus. Since their job is to make the company succeed, you could use share options and a bonus plan to link their income to the company's performance. Share options should be aligned with long-term performance, while bonuses and profit-sharing should be based on the past year's results.

Of course, not all executives crave shares. Ideally, you'd probably someone capable who's happy with a challenging job and modest salary. And these people are out there! More now than ever.

Some well-qualified people care more about family time, a fun culture, a challenging job, or being part of a world-changing business, i.e., yours. The more you understand each person's drivers and values, the more you can craft deals that satisfy them in ways that transcend status and money.

If you are giving shares away, you will need professional help, as mentioned earlier. You are likely to regret not doing so within the foreseeable future intensely.

- Delegating to your new team (don't abdicate)

As each of the new members of your team comes on board, it's time for the truly challenging part: trusting them.

Your gut instinct will fight you every step of the way. You will assume your instructions are clear and misunderstandings are their fault. You will believe when you disagree that you're right and they're wrong. However, you will often be wrong more than you are right; after all, they are the professionals in their area.

A primary key to successful executive relationships is changing what your gut tells you. Why is this? Your 'gut' instinct is a result of your experiences. Unless you have experienced a great deal of hiring and firing senior management teams, your 'gut' does not have the necessary experience. You will learn this over time; however, in-between times, we suggest that you tapped into an experienced advisor such as your coach and Mentor.

Remember how you interviewed for trust? That's critical because once you hire your dream team, you must let them take their responsibilities and run with them. That means agreeing with them about their roles, what deliverables they're responsible for, and over what timeframe.

It's essential to decide in advance how you will handle the inevitable disagreements. You hired this person assuming their knowledge, experience, and judgment were better than yours. So when you disagree, if you did you picked the right team member, it's more likely that they are right and you are wrong. Discuss early on how you will make the call to get the most benefit from the situation. Just remember: If you agree on everything, one of you is now redundant, and hopefully that is you!

Outstanding entrepreneurship is about going for goals that are much bigger than what you could achieve alone. Your job isn't to reach the destination; it's to build your dream team that will reach these goals.

If you want to reach your goals, you'll need to recruit your dream team to help. Creating a world-class dream team means knowing what you want them to do, finding the best candidates, and supplying them with what they need to do their jobs well. If you choose wisely, they'll be successful and help you reach your goals. Your Mentor should be able to help you.

Exercise

Write down your thoughts on building your dream team. You may need your coach or Mentor to help you with this exercise.

26. Funding your Growth

G rowing your enterprise will require an increased amount of working capital to *fund* your growth.

Having insufficient working capital in your business is likely to dramatically reduce your profits, increase your risk of failure and create unnecessary levels of stress.

Top Tip Funding is not a luxury; it is critical to creating high levels of sustainable growth.

This section explains your funding options in detail.

The six main methods of increasing your working capital.

1. Your own money.
2. Your profits.
3. Your friends and family's money.
4. Other People's Money (OPM)
5. Selling your shares.
6. Free money.

You can use the funding for pretty much any purpose.

- Employ more staff.
- Take on key players to create your team

- Increase your marketing spend.

- Buy in professional help to grow your business.

- To be able to buy more stock.

- Fit-out your shops, warehouse, office, etc

- Buy computers and other costly kits.

- To pay your VAT or Tax bill.

- Pay for staff training.

- To buy or lease your company cars.

- To buy more machinery.

- Open up further outlets/ shops /offices.

- Pay off higher-risk lending such as an overdraft.

- To buy another company

Your own money

- **Your Savings**

We believe that you should use your own money to ***part-fund*** your growing business during the start-up phase.

It would be best to sell assets that you don't need to fund your business.

We also believe that you must personally feel the pain of spending your own money for the first few months.

Secondly, you should not ask others to invest or lend their money to your business without first investing your own money.

Top Tip You should only use a modest proportion of your funds to finance your business.

We believe that you should retain a safety net of savings, just in case things don't go to plan.

Having cash set aside should also ensure that you make sounder business decisions. This is because you are likely to be more relaxed and less emotional when making important decisions.

Your Business Profits

Using your profits exclusively to fund your business is often referred to as 'Bootstrapping' or 'growing organically.'

We applaud Bootstrapping for the first six months or so. Frankly, if you can't make your business work using your funds, you are unlikely to be successful using other people's money.

After 6 to 12 months, exclusively 'Bootstrapping', your business is likely to bring your growth to a halt. Before this point, raising funds via other people to fuel your growth is critical.

Top Tip, A *successful* entrepreneur would never advise you to Bootstrap.

Top Tip 2. Successful entrepreneurs will also tell you that your profits should be used to increase your personal wealth rather than to fund your business. That's why they are rich, and you are not (yet).

- **Pension Backed Funding**

Pension Backed Funding (PBF) is proving increasingly popular.

PBF entails setting up a SSAS company pension scheme, where the founders are the only members. With our help, you then transfer some or all of your old pension schemes into it.

The SSAS may then lend up to 50% of the fund's value to your own business. Rates are typically around 1.5%-2% pa over 5 years. As the Trustee, you make this decision.

EG If you transfer £200,000 from your old pensions into the SSAS you can invest up to £100,000 into your own business. This is your call.

Top Tip Many suggest that this form of funding should only be used in conjunction with funding from elsewhere.

Top Tip 2 It is often advised that companies should only ever use PBF with a strong management team and support.

If you wish to set up a SSAS loan, The Growth Gurus have almost a decade of experience.

- Your Friends and Families Money

If you have a truly great idea and you have proven your model, then we encourage you to look to your friends and family to raise a proportion of the funds your business needs.

If you later wish to raise funds from a business angel, they are likely to expect you initially raised money from your friends and family. Why should they invest in you if you have not invested yourself?

Raising funds from your family is also likely to keep you even more motivated and focused on succeeding. After all, you don't want to let your family down, do you?

It may help to create a formal agreement with your family for any loans or investments. We can help you with this.

Top Tip Please don't ask for more money than you know your relatives can afford to lose!

Top Tip 2: You should only ask for money from friends and family until you have utilised your savings.

Other People's Money (OPM)

- **The Start Up Loan Company (SUL)**

If you have been trading for less than two years, you could access up to £25k per director from the Start-Up Loan Company.

Even if you have a mature business, you may be able to access these funds.

The Start-Up Loan Company is a Government-backed body set up to help Start-Ups. A Start-Up loan is a personal loan with rates of less than 6% and payable over 5 years.

We can support you with the process, including helping with your Business plan.

Top Tip. Please don't overestimate your potential sales and underestimate your potential costs. You may benefit from taking some advice on your financial projections, something we can also help with.

We support directors just like you to obtain a start-up loan.

- **Business Loan**

As the name implies, a business loan gives you the funds you need, and you pay these back with interest.

Each funder has its criteria, and these vary considerably. This makes sourcing the ideal provider almost impossible for any business owner without support from a finance expert.

Several funders require your business to be profitable, yet your turnover is more important than others.

Rates vary from 5% pa, and loan periods can vary from a few months to five years.

The great news is that some loans can be processed in less than 48 hours.

Top Tip. It is vital that you carefully choose 4 or 5 of our 200 lenders and focus on them. The rest are likely to either be (a) inappropriate for your business and (b) likely to turn you down.

Top Tip 2 Just because a funder is willing to back you does not mean that you should agree.

- **Regional Growth Funds**

Most regions in the UK have Regional Growth Funds, and you should be able to access these funds if your business resides in these areas.

The interest rates are typically much lower than commercial funders, and as a result, we believe that Regional Growth Funds should be one of your first options.

- **Invoice Discounting**

Invoice discounting enables you to be paid from your invoice before the invoices are due to be paid.

You should be able to select which invoices you need to be financed to give you **part** of the working capital you require.

Top Tip. Most financial experts suggest that this form of funding is used (a) selectively and (b) only when you are growing your sales quickly, and (c) should only form a part of your funding strategy.

- **Bridging**

This type of funding is known as 'Bridging' because it's designed as a short-term solution for your business.

You can also use Bridging when buying or refurbishing property as well as growth capital.

Rates vary considerably and are dependent on many factors. Expect to pay more than twice the rate you pay for longer-term secured loans.

Top Tip. Don't be tempted to overuse Bridging when less costly options are available.

- **Asset Finance**

Asset finance enables you to finance assets you need to run your business. Asset finance avoids the need to use your precious cash. After all, it would help if you had the money within your business and not tied up in assets.

Assets can include, Furniture and white goods, office equipment, vehicles, machinery, etc.

You can also refinance the assets that your business already owns to raise the funds you need.

Asset finance may cover all of these areas;

- **Refurbishments** – Furniture, ceilings, flooring, lighting, partitioning, security
- **Vehicles** – Cars, Vans, HGV, Fork-Lifts, Trailers. (Business & Personal Finance)
- **Plant & Machinery** – All Yellow Plant and Construction Machinery

- **Engineering & Manufacturing Equipment** - Production lines etc.

- **IT Equipment** – All Hardware & Software (Including Annual Subscriptions)

- **Office Equipment** –Printers, Photocopiers, Telephone Systems, Furniture.

As with any other form of funding, there are many providers, and their rates and criteria vary considerably.

- **Overdrafts**

An overdraft is the most common form of business funding for small businesses; however it's also the highest risk, likely to be painfully expensive and highly addictive.

Overdrafts can be withdrawn or reduced with little or no notice and should only ever form a modest part of your funding mix.

Top Tip If most of your funding is based on an overdraft facility, you should call us immediately.

We have witnessed hundreds of excellent businesses fail because they relied too heavily on their overdraft, and the facility was withdrawn without any reason.

- **Trade Finance**

If your business buys from overseas, then you could benefit from Trade Finance.

Trade Finance funders pay overseas suppliers on your behalf to enable the import of goods into the UK.

They will often fund up to 100% of the landed cost of stock, including VAT, Duty, and Freight charges.

Funders often pay deposits to suppliers before the manufacture of products.

We have access to all the Trade Finance providers in the UK and can source the ideal funder for you.

- **Stock Finance**

Stock Finance is designed for companies who hold a great deal of stock to ensure that they can always supply their customers quickly.

Firm orders for the onward sale of stock are not always possible in today's commercial environment.

There are only a few stock finance providers with rates and criteria varying considerably. We have access to all the Stock Finance providers in the UK and can source the ideal funder for you.

To Recap

Most highly successful businesses tend to use a combination of most of these funding options.

Throughout your businesses development, the proportions of each funding method will need to change.

The challenge is getting the balance right.

We have yet to meet a successful business that has not fully taken advantage of Other People's Money!

27. Selling your Shares to raise Funds

Private Equity Investment

This form of funding entails sourcing investors willing to invest money into your business in exchange for shares.

Many believe that raising money by selling your shares should only be considered if you have no choice.

You will be selling your shares one day, and selling a proportion very early in your development may result in you regretting the decision when you realise that the shares you traded in the early days are now worth £millions.

What can be even more upsetting are the restrictions often placed upon your activity. Let's face it, selling shares means you lose some or a great deal of control of your business.

Private Equity investment is a great idea when your debt funding options are limited.

Private Equity Investment comes under many names; Angel, VC, and EIS fund.

You will need to prepare well if you wish to attract investors. You will need to create a business plan and Deck that will be appealing to investors.

If appropriate, you will need to seek pre-approval from the HMRC to gain SEIS or EIS status.

SEIS and EIS is a scheme where the investor receives a considerable tax benefit. Having SEIS or EIS status will often improve your investment provider options.

Top Tip You will need to pitch your business to investors at several pitching events. Preparing for this takes expert tuition so that when you pitch to investors, you will put across a great message to increase the chance of an investor deciding to invest in you and your business.

Top Tip. Business Angels are not always as angelic as we would want them to be. Many Angels may have nefarious reasons for investing in your business. Such investors may create traps that may result in them taking over your business.

Crowdfunding

Crowd Funding is a form of equity finance and can raise considerable amounts of money; however, raising the money is likely to be both challenging and very time-consuming.

Preparation is key to raising money with Crowdfunding, and the whole process will take at least six months. This is contrary to what most platforms may tell you.

That's possibly because you pay them to list on their site, and they have no interest in telling you that raising funds on a Crowdfunding site is very hard work.

One of the other downsides of CrowdFunding is that it will lose a proportion of your shares.

One other negative aspect is that you are showcasing your excellent business idea to thousands of people, and you may find yourself with a competitor copying your business model.

If you are happy to spend a great deal of your time dealing with a raise with a Crowd Funder and you don't mind giving away equity, then Crowd Funding may be perfect for you.

Free Money

- **R and D Claims**

An often-overlooked method to create a proportion of the growth funds you require is a Research and Development (R and D) claim.

The average claim for a client is £40,000, and you do not need to sell your precious shares or repay the money.

If you have developed your process, systems, or products, you could benefit from a Research and Development claim.

This may result in your business receiving a cheque from the HMRC, even if you have not paid them anything.

There are many consultants in the market to choose from, and the Growth Gurus have a panel of the most experienced.

- **Grants**

Securing grant funding could help your business develop and grow. However, even experts can find it challenging to keep track of the hundreds of different grant schemes, which keep appearing and disappearing.

You need to identify relevant grant schemes and understand whether your business is likely to qualify. You also have to understand the application process and decide whether it is worth applying.

You must be ready to put up some of your own money.

Grants typically cover 15-60% of the total finance required for a project. It is rare for a grant to finance 100% of the costs of any project.

Even if a more significant proportion of the project cost is available, you will still need to invest time and resources in researching and applying for the grant.

There are many Grant consultants in the market to choose from, and the Growth Gurus have a panel of the most experienced.

28. Don't forget you, your family, and your health.

———◦◦◦———

M any business owners will foolishly attempt to work 24 hours a day, 7 days a week, 365 days per year if allowed to get away with it. They will ignore their sanity, their health, and their friends. Last but not least, their families may start to be treated as an afterthought.

On the other hand, a real entrepreneur would create a true balance in their business and personal life.

Business founders often forget why they set up the business in the first place. They become obsessed with the business. We meet this type of small business owner all the time, and in 2015 two of them died because of their obsession.

I have been guilty of this many times. I often become super obsessed. It's only because of my team that I can pull myself out of this.

Changing an obsession is much easier said than done. If you are blind to your family's needs, your health, and those around you, you are suffering a common affliction that will only ever end in tears. I want to help you gain more balance, and it's never too late to start (Have you seen Scrooge?)

We strongly suggest that you find some form of balance, or you will fail on several levels. Find your 'Why'

Simon Sinek has written an excellent book called. Finding your Why, and we recommend this book as one of your first books to read to help you.

First of all, it is vital that you grasp the following concept that may be alien to you....

Your business is not a separate part of your life; it's part of the integrated whole.

If you are out of sync in one area, you won't experience the true meaning and fulfillment we all yearn for as humans.

In practical terms, you need to give expression to your purpose in a balanced way in all the areas of your life.

This encompasses:

- Your relationship with yourself, including your physical, emotional, and spiritual health and wellbeing,
- Your relationship with others, including family and friends.
- Your relationship with the world, including your business and pro bono work.

    To help you with this we need to deal with three distinct steps:

- Your core values
- Set your personal goals; and
- Create a personal as well as a business action plan
- Write a Business Plan for your Life as well as your Business!

To live a balanced business life and ensure your long-term success on every level, you need to set both business and personal goals. Business owners often don't consider the connection between business and personal goals, which can often create dissidence between the two elements of your life.

Ideally, when setting up a business, you should consider your personal goals first. However, most don't!

First off, we suggest that you set up goals for yourself.

Your fitness will directly affect your business performance, and we encourage you to have a balanced focus on your health. If you like going to the Gym then factor your Gym visits into your diary. Source yourself as an excellent fitness coach as well.

If you feel that you don't have the time, just remember that you will need to factor in time for illness if you don't make time for fitness.

The amount of hours you work is essential. Studies strongly suggest that 'working' over 50 hours per week is counterproductive. If you spend 12 hour days in the office all week and then work another 10 hours at the weekend, your performance will likely be less than if you had only worked 8 hours a day for 5 days.

Many business owners also end up eating all the wrong types of food at the wrong times. If you now find yourself 50 lb's overweight, set up some goals to get back to your fighting weight.

Your mental health is as equally important as your physical health. Everyone is different, of course. I find it easier to take very long walks that helps me both physically and mentally. Many of my best ideas often come about on long walks with my dogs. To paraphrase Friedrich Nietzsche.

Factor in specific goals for spending time with the family. You could even combine this with walking the dog!

Setting days when the family eats at the same table with no phones, Ipads etc is excellent on many levels.

Remember, if these are goals, you need to write all of this down and give yourself specific dates and times.

If your business takes you away from home, factor in a goal for how many days you will stay at home and days where your family comes to you. Your family may love the idea of a road trip to where you are.

Once your business has started to grow, you may consider some pro bono work. You could even consider mentoring some young entrepreneurs just setting out!

Goal setting is challenging, and you may benefit from employing the services of a professional coach to tease your actual goals out. It's incredible to watch someone come alive when working with a qualified and experienced coach or mentor.

To Recap

- Your life and business are the same.
- A misaligned 'work life balance' is counterproductive, and you will feel less whole as a result.
- Look to balance every aspect of your life. Too much of any one area will often lead to stress and failure in others.
- There are three main elements to consider; You, others, and the world.

As with any other area in your life, define your values, set the goals as you do with business, create the action plan and then go for it!

Exercise.

What are you going to do to improve the balance in your life?

You may wish to ask your coach to help you with this.

29. Life time Learning

The majority of successful entrepreneurs acknowledge that much of their success is down to educating themselves.

They set themselves daily targets for reading, watching, or listening to educational YouTube videos, masterclasses, etc.

They diarise these times; they often create a special space for reading.

I listen to YouTube videos for at least 10 hours per week when walking the dogs and another 5 hours while driving the car or traveling on the train. That's 15 hours of education per week, 750 hours per year.

I truly believe that reading and listening to good quality material gives you a form of hindsight. You could even call it retrospective hindsight. Consuming the lives, the successes, the failures, and the ideas of others will give you the benefit of their experiences.

I believe that understanding other people's ideas create ideas of your own.

I will state with conviction that over 50% of my more considerable mistakes in the first 15 years of business would have been avoided if I had read more of the books in our suggested reading list. I would conservatively put the cost of those mistakes at over $10million.

Not educating myself enough earlier in my life is one of my only regrets.

I have compiled a reading list for you:

1. Rich Dad, Poor Dad - Robert Kiyosaki

2. Mindset- Dr. Carol Dwek

3. Finding your Why. Simon Sinek

4. Key Person of Influence. Daniel Priestley

5. The E Myth - Michael Gerber

6. The Morning Miracle- Hal Elrod.

7. How to win friends and Influence People-Dale Carnegie

8. The Power of Positive Thinking - Norman Vincent Peale

9. The 7 Habits of Highly Effective People - Stephen Covey

10. The Richest Man in Babylon - George C. Clason

11. Leaders Eat Last- Simon Sinek

12. Find Your Why-Simon Sinek

13. The Bankers Code - George Antone

14. The Wealth Code - George Antone

15. Mind & Emotions - George Zelucki

16. Feel the Fear and do it anyway - Susan Jeffers

17. The Mac Anderson series of books

18. Goals - Zig Ziglar

19. Law of Attraction - Esta Hicks

20. The Best Year Ever - Jim Rohn

21. The Art of Exceptional Living - Jim Rohn

22. The Automatic Millionaire - David Bach

23. The Way of the Peaceful Warrior - Dan Milman

24. The Power of Now - Eckhart Tolle

25. The Cashflow Quadrant - Rober Kiyosaki

26. How to have a superpower memory - Harry Lorraine

27. Think & Grow Rich - Napoleon Hill

28. The Slight Edge - Jeff Olson

29. Daring Greatly - Brené Brown

30. Five Pieces to The Life Puzzle' - Jim Rohn

31. The Magic of Thinking Big - David J. Schwartz

32. Living An Abundant Life - Sandy Foster

33. Breaking The Habit Of Being Yourself - Dr Joe Dispenza

34. The Secret - Rhonda Byrne

35. As A Man Thinketh - James Allen

36. You Were Born Rich - Bob Proctor

37. Beermat Entrepreneur - Mike Southern

38. You Are A Badass - Jen Sincero

39. Outwitting The Devil - Napoleon Hill

40. The Subtle Art Of Not Giving A F*UK - Mark Manson

41. The Motivation Manifesto - Brendan Burchard

42. The Compound Effect - Darren Hardy

43. The Laptop Millionaire - Mark Anastasi

44. Think Yourself Rich - Joseph Murphy

45. Dare to Dream Work To Win - Dr Tom Barrett

46. The Language of Letting Go - Melody Beattie

47. More Language of Letting Go - Melody Beattie

48. The millionaire Mindset - T Harv Eker

49. Money and the Law of Attraction - Esther and Jerry Hicks

50. FU Money- Dan Lok

"All readers are not leaders, yet all leaders are readers".

- Harry Truman.

I often read books two or three times, with sometimes years between each read. I have just finished "7 Habits of Highly Effective People" for the third time in 20 years. I buy a new version each time I read the book and make notes as I read. My library has books festooned with little tabs!

If you find yourself in the car a great deal, then maybe you could buy audiobooks? Just go to Amazon or any other high-end retailer to source material.

You could even listen to YouTube. Type In the details of whom you wish to listen to and press go! You could use the reading list as a guide? I spend up to 50% of my time walking the dogs, while in the car, on trains and planes listening to educational stuff on YouTube. That equates to over 2 hours per day, 365 days per year, over 700 hours over the year, or around 80 working days, purely educating myself.

Attend courses at least once every two months. I try and attend a course at least once per month and love learning new things and widening my horizons. I even attend courses on business growth at my local universities, where I tend to annoy the lecturers (who typically have no experience of creating and running a business). I still pick up a thing or two, and that's what matters most.

Learn a new skill that's not business-focused. Gaining business knowledge is vital; however, please consider attending courses to learn a new skill with nothing to do with your business. This could be very therapeutic and may even be quite handy.

A very wealthy client recently learned to lay bricks, and at first, I could not think why! This week I wanted to build a brick bbq and then wished that I had also attended.

To Recap.

1. To speed up your growth, learn from others.

2. Learning from other people's mistakes is nearly as effective as making a mistake yourself. Consuming other people's ideas and experiences allows you to 'virtually' make thousands of errors a year without the cost.

3. The more ideas you consume, the more ideas that you will have.

Exercise

Write down what you are going to do to learn first.

You may need to work with your coach or mentor to refine this.

30. Growing your Wealth

Business owners often focus so much energy on their business finances that they forget to build their wealth.

A true Entrepreneur would create a financial balance between their enterprises and their wealth.

To be truly successful, you need to start buying income-producing Assets for you and your family outside of the business, and you need to create this habit the day you open your business.

To enable this to happen, you need:

- Your business to create an increasing amount of profit, part of which you can draw out of the business to enhance your wealth.

- You must realise that you need to take a proportion of the company's money and put this away within safe investments outside of your business, even if you believe that you need the money in the business.

- You may need to replace your cash within the business with business loans and investments to achieve the above.

- You need to pay yourself first, and this may entail raising the money your company needs from elsewhere.

Many of our truly successful clients make regular payments from their companies into investments within a pension fund and income-producing Assets, and they do this almost from day one. They have made paying themselves a primary strategy and part of the business process. This means that they do not need to think about creating their wealth on a day-to-day basis. Building their wealth then becomes part of 'the system.'

We have witnessed that our more successful clients often 'live under their means,' investing up to 70% of their profits and spending the rest.

They use business loans and investments to fund growth and release the profit in their business to build their wealth.

We have discovered that many unsuccessful business owners retain most of their profits within the company and use their money for working capital instead of raising funds from elsewhere.

We meet business owners every day who are proud of their achievements and are pleased that they have achieved so much with limited amounts of lending. Admittedly, many of these businesses appear to be successful and have made $millions, yet they often have very little personal investment as a family.

They are often proud of 'Bootstrapping' their business, a method that has kept them poor! We believe that this is simply a flawed mindset.

I was guilty of this way of thinking during my first business. Even after we had made the first £1m in profits, I had still not taken out £1 to start building my wealth. Would I do the same again? No, of course not.

A small number of people go into business to build up a valuable business and then sell to the highest bidder. Some genuinely believe that reinvesting all their profit is the best way. However, this is a seriously flawed philosophy.

This philosophy is flawed on several levels;

- Creating wealth by investing your profits enables you to make actual income that is not derived from your trading business. You can start to create an income source with almost no effort.

Over a while, your investment income could create enough income that you are financially independent of your business.

Can you imagine this? Can you imagine the freedom you would feel when you no longer need to worry about where your income is coming from?

You could, of course, continue with developing the business you founded or could decide to sell on your shares, creating even more money to invest.

Millions of people have achieved this form of financial freedom, and if you follow our guidance, you too could do the same.

- One day you may wish to sell your shares and exit from the business. Having money put aside outside of your business gives you a considerable degree of leverage. Having a few $million already in your coffers will enable you to walk away from deals that you should walk away from. The buyers will also know that you have personal wealth, and they will realise that they cannot bully you into accepting a poor deal.

We have seen many business owners who have come to us too late, who have already sold their business because they had to, not because they wanted to.

This is because they have not invested enough in building their team alongside the systems the business needs, and their excuse is often "we did not have enough money." The classic bu**s**t "We wanted to grow organically."

- 97% of companies fail within ten years, and business owners seldom plan for this to happen of course.

Naturally, if they have transferred a few $million away into pensions and other investment vehicles over the lifetime of the business, then a failure of the business would be far less painful.

Imagine the countless business owners who have built a business using just their own money and are left destitute because of business failure. The number suffering this fate is in the millions.

Would you please make sure you adopt a strategy to build up your wealth to create financial freedom? Adopt this strategy from day one, even if you only invest just a few £ per day.

We strongly recommend that you put at least 20% to 70% of the profit away and out of easy reach when your business makes a profit. The amount will depend on the level of profit, of course. The more you make, the more you can invest.

In the UK, a SSAS trust is one of the ideal vehicles for this purpose. You can invest up to £1m of your profits into your Trust, and 100% of the money you invest is free of tax. So, for example, if you are investing £5000 of your profits per month, you won't have to pay tax on these profits. If you had kept the funds within your business, then you would have paid corporation tax. If you had then paid the remaining money to yourself, then you would pay tax as well.

Apart from the considerable tax benefits, the cash you have put away into a SSAS can be put to several uses unavailable to all other pensions;

- 50% of the gross value can be lent straight back to your company, and all the interest is paid back into the SSAS, tax-free. Think about this for a little while. You would have paid around 45% of the money in tax if you had not put the cash into the SSAS.

- You can buy commercial property with the money, even the building you use. Your SSAS can buy some or all of the property. Keep in mind that the SSAS is buying with Gross money, which means that a proportion of the cash would normally have been paid to the HMRC. This means that the taxman is helping you to buy property!

- All of the money in the SSAS is protected from creditors if your business or even you become insolvent.

- You can sell various assets of the company, including your Intellectual property, to your SSAS. If your business fails, then your SSAS will own some of your more essential assets enabling you to restart the next day again, renting your assets from your pension scheme. This is of considerable benefit for companies who have a fixed and floating charge over all the company's assets where insolvency would typically result in a 'pre pack.'

A SSAS may help you avoid many of the issues and challenges faced in this event and may allow the directors to re-start a business much more easily and quickly. (please see some detail on this later in this chapter)

- All the funds and assets in your SSAS fall outside your estate for IHT planning. We all die one day, and a serious issue facing the children of wealthy people is IHT. At least with a SSAS, you have £3m within the Trusts; rather than paying £1.2m in IHT, your children pay £0 on these assets and, more importantly, they can utilise these assets without the need to go through probate. Probate can take years and is only complete when the IHT is paid.

This is not financial advice. My suggestions here are what I have found work for those who have built up their wealth and become financially free.

We recommend that you engage with a suitably experienced FCA-regulated IFA to seek advice and guidance when investing to increase your wealth. Selecting your ideal IFA can be a challenge, and you should seek references. I also believe that you should only take on an IFA with considerable experience in handling the wealth of business founders.

If you don't put an agreed proportion of your profits out of immediate reach, you will likely experience 'lifestyle creep.'

Lifestyle creep is the scenario where your household expenses track your earnings: a bigger house, second house, bigger car, another car, bigger this, more of that. I did this for ten years plus, and while it was fun, the policy does not bring about any stability for your family. It doesn't create financial freedom.

I was very guilty of this. At 28, my drawings were around £2,000 per month, and within two years, they had crept up to £10,000 and two years later, £20,000. I was only ever investing circa 1% of my profits. It seems stupid when you read this. I have met countless business founders who have done the same.

Truly Wealthy People Invest first and live off the rest. Poor People spend their money and invest what's left.

Many founders have put money into property, and that has proven beneficial for millions of business owners for hundreds of years and is likely to carry on being a sound long-term method of building your wealth.

Many others have invested their money into various Forex Funds, Stocks, shares, Commodities such as Gold, etc.

In my opinion, you should invest over a broad spectrum of asset classes.

My favourite is Forex because the average income per fund I am in is 10% per month. Even though this has been the case for over 12 years, I still only have 10% of my wealth in Forex. We are happy to share our strategies with you.

I have many friends who no longer need to run a business or work because their income from their property investments gives them considerable income. They are now financially free.

One friend, who has just turned 40, hardly ever saw his parents as a child because they were 'busy .' He vowed that this would not happen to him. He has three young children, and every 8-week summer holiday, the whole family goes and stays in their villa, exploring Europe. They go away every other school holiday as well. They visit Disney at least twice per year and Lapland in December.

What a magical life for him, his life partner, and his children, and you can quickly achieve this as well. Just following my book would help; joining one of our Mastermind groups would be even better.

So How do financially free business founders create their wealth?

One of the methods used by many wealthy entrepreneurs to extract cash from their companies is to stop using their own cash to fund the growth of the business. They view the use of their funds as a high-risk investment. They then invest their profits outside of the business to grow their wealth.

Many founders replace the funds they take out of the business with funds the company borrows.

While there is interest to pay, which reduces profits very slightly, at least the funds are now in your possession rather than being used as working capital.

These entrepreneurs don't take out all the profit, just enough to build up their wealth. Typically we have found that these entrepreneurs funneled 20%-70% of profits straight into investments, with 50% being paid out as dividends to fund their lifestyle, school fees, and liabilities, with the rest remaining in the business.

I mentioned how a SSAS may help you re start a business after a failure.

A SSAS is a trust, and if the SSAS owns company assets, you as the Trustee can then rent the assets back to your new company straight away. So your SSAS may own your premises, your website, your data, all your IP, etc. Of course, you will need to take professional advice; however, I am sure you will see why wealthy business founders so well like SSAS.

To Recap

- To be financially free and independent of your business for your income, you need to invest a proportion of your profits into assets that produce an income. I.e., property, Forex trading, share trading.

- You should invest first and then live off what's left

- The money can be paid directly from your company into a SSAS trust without the need to pay tax on the money.

- Buying the building your company operates from by using your SSAS is often a great way to start to build up your wealth.

- Using property to accrue your wealth is a common method used by many.

- There are many ways of investing your profits in creating financial freedom, and you may wish to utilise a qualified and experienced IFA to help you. We are happy to share how we did it.

- There are only two ways that you exit a business; it fails, or you sell. Either way, you will be glad that you have created an investment fund for your family.

Exercise

Write down what you are going to do to increase your wealth outside of your business.

Request a call with me to discover how we achieved financial freedom.

31. Ensuring That Your Company Thrives Beyond ten years.

To ensure success over the medium and long term, you need to avoid these two pitfalls

1. You only do much of the same thing (exploitation of your current assets).

2. You only do what is new (exploration to discover new assets).

The real solution to long-term growth is to continually figure out a balance between these two activities continually and do so every month of every year that you lead your business.

There is no time in human history has it been more important to focus on this activity. If you are not innovating, then your business is effectively dead already.

Instilling this Mindset within your culture will pay dividends for years and is likely to enable your business to last for decades or longer.

This balancing act is equally important in your first two years because too much of either will bring a swift end to your enterprise.

Balancing between exploration and exploitation is even more critical for your long-term success because if you falter at any stage, this will have severe ramifications for your company's longevity.

Both exploitation and exploration are necessary; however, too much of either will often lead to failure, especially the more mature your business becomes.

Consider Kodak as an example. Kodak was one of the biggest companies in the world, and they dominated printed film. A small division of Kodak invented the digital camera. The Kodak Board of Directors was given a report stating that the digital camera would make film obsolete within 15 to 20 years.

The Board decided to carry on exploiting film instead of exploring this new system.

Within a couple of years, this massive company had vanished because they failed to explore this new opportunity.

Too much exploration can also bring a company down. We have often seen this in young companies with a CEO who was always exploring new ideas and did not have a strong enough team around them to force the exploitation of these great ideas. These businesses spent too much energy and resources exploring new avenues to forget to exploit the ones they had.

I met one of these in Nov 2017. The company had created an App' that had global potential. The app worked, and it was straightforward to use, so it was ready to scale. Their investors engaged us to see if we could help.

It turned out that the founder was busy 10 hours per day with the developers rather than selling the space to the advertisers, i.e., its only income source. He had forgotten that the app needed to make money. This was crazy, and we sent him out to sell the product. The business soon after collapsed; what a waste.

The moral of this story is simple. You will never reach perfection, and if you relish perfection, you will just need to live with this fact. Develop the product to exceed expectations by 10%, not 1000%; 10% is good enough for now; just make sure that it's always 10%. Then exploit the service you have created, gradually improving it while exploring for the next giant leap.

Exploration is not just about coming up with what's new. It's about searching and discovering the new. It's about new products and innovation. It's about challenging and then changing the frontiers. Dreaming beyond your current reality.

Our heroes are often famous because of their exploration: Sir Edmund Hillary, Neil Armstrong, Scot of the Antarctic etc.

We all know that exploration is a high risk, and it's exciting!

We don't know the answers; we don't know if we will find out what the answers are and understand that the risks are high, so high that we might die or our company could fail.

Exploitation is the opposite of exploration.

Exploitation is knowing the systems or products we already have and simply making them better slowly over time. We exploit the services you currently offer by systemising the operation to such an extent that the company becomes systems dependent, which is a good thing.

Exploitation is about increasing our revenue per client each year by improving the service provision. It's about making all of your products or services faster, cheaper, better…Exploitation is not risky….in the medium to long term; however, pure exploitation becomes increasingly high risk the further we look into the future. So if your company only relies on exploitation, this policy is very high risk in the long term and is likely to lead to business failure.

If you want to witness your company lasting 10, 20, 30 or even 100 years, your business also needs to explore. If you're going to just look at the short term, you might focus only on exploitation.

Some markets are ideal for exploitation only. These are markets with a short lifespan of just a year or two. You would, of course, be wise to invest profits into exploration to find the next market opportunity or the asset you built will need to be dismantled once this market has been mined.

I have two small daughters, Pippa, 5, Alice, 8, and they explore all day. They have minimal resources to exploit. As my children grow older, they will explore less because they will have more knowledge. I will, of course, be there whispering in their ear and encouraging them to explore and try things that scare them a little.

The same goes for your company. As your company matures, it will become less exploratory, less innovative as you and your team become more competent with your current business model.

You, the founder, alongside your whole management team, must be acutely aware of the 'success' trap. You need to run your company efficiently, yet you also need to reinvent it, or your company will fail. Make sure that you have explored enough and changed enough that you don't become obsolete.

Even Apple would have failed if they had kept the original iPhone; Samsung would now be king.

Nokia is an example of a failure to explore. Nokia dominated the world's market and even came up with the first 'iPhone. However, they failed to explore enough, and they are now close to bankruptcy.

Building your business is challenging; creating a balance between exploitation and exploration is an art. You will need to use outside coaches and mentors to retain the balance over the years. This is one of the main reasons why the vast majority of successful long-term businesses have independent professionals, often taking the form of Mentors, Business Coaches or Non-Exec Directors or both.

Please don't delude yourself that your accountant can help you explore. It's not in their nature to explore, so don't ask them to help you develop this Mindset, this system.

Only a small fraction of growth companies are able to explore and exploit at the same time effectively. I estimate that the number will be somewhere around 1-2%. With this 2%, the payoffs are enormous. In the larger business world, we have plenty of examples.

We have Apple going into phones, Tesla creating electric cars, Nestle creating Nespresso, Lego going into animated films, Toyota creating their Hybrid cars. There are lots more examples, and the benefits to these companies are considerable. The same goes for smaller companies that are growing.

Why is this balancing act so difficult?

When a company is within its first few years, exploration is the main focus. However, as the company becomes systemised and familiar with its market, the business can rapidly shift to just focusing on exploitation. They forget to explore. Unless they fully embrace exploration, they will quickly become obsolete. They will stagnate and inevitably fail unless they realise that they still need to commit resources to explore.

Demanding shareholders can force a company to focus on exploitation. However, as a Director, it is your legal and moral duty to educate these shareholders that this is a short-term solution.

This is when the founder needs to step away from leading the business's day-to-day activity and focus on exploration. This does depend on the personality type of the founder, and another key member of the management team may be best suited to the role of exploration. If you have a mentor or coach, then you can discuss this issue with them.

After all, this is what happened at Apple with Steve Jobs, and look where this got them!

One of the other reasons for lack of balance is when the management team doesn't have the patience to let new products or services flourish.

There is a common habit of creating a new service, trying it for a short time, and then replacing it. This is where the exploitation team (Operations typically) have too much control over the new project. This is especially relevant for companies who have adopted 'lean working' as a method of operation.

The team or individual who comes up with all the great ideas will become frustrated and demoralised and eventually give up or leave. This is why I started my first business.

One of the other traps for a business is the success trap. This is very common, and I suffered from this myself, and it cost me $millions.

As Bill Gates once said;

"Success is a lousy teacher; it seduces us into thinking that we cannot fail."

I have found that companies who have become amazingly good at what they do if they are operationally centered on exploitation, the leadership team tends to shun new ideas; they ignore exploration. They fail soon after.

We understand that when we do anything well, it can be almost impossible to change. What we all need in this situation is someone to challenge our thinking, our perspective. This person is often a coach or a mentor, an outspoken chairman. Joining a Mastermind Group to challenge you as well as support your ideas is a fantastic idea.

For a values-driven business keeping a balance between exploitation and exploration is much easier to do. Values don't change, and it's easier to get back on track because by only exploiting, you will soon shift away from your values, the 'why' you are in business. That said, you still need someone independent to challenge you and the Board.

Here are a few lessons to consider;

1. Be ahead of the crisis. Companies that can explore are adding security for the future.

2. Keep multiple time scales in your mind and within your planning. For a mature business, exploration makes very little difference in the value and profits of the current year. However, as the years roll forward, the products or services born out of the exploration will become a considerable element of your company's income.

3. Invite someone to challenge you and your Board. It is challenging to balance exploitation and exploration in our minds or even within a management team. Creating balance is a team sport, and we all need a coach to encourage this balance. You could also rely on your Mastermind group.

4. Don't be seduced by success. As your company becomes successful, it is easy to fall into the trap of believing your BS. This is where a great coach or mentor can whisper in your ear

as you receive the adoration, the awards, the large dividend cheques, "You are only human," or Memento Homo. Again, being part of a Mastermind Group will help considerably.

5. Take part in a Mastermind group of other business owners and entrepreneurs, which will help you be accountable to others. Still, more importantly, you can gain new ideas that can help you explore new ways of your business to move forwards and innovate.

With regards to your own company, here are a few questions to ask yourself.

1. What parts of your company have started to delude themselves because they are successful? Are they now on some form of 'auto pilot'?

2. As the founder, what can you do to challenge the increasingly embedded status quo?

3. To take the management team out of their slumber?

After all, they are sleepwalking your business over the edge of a cliff. This may not happen this year; however, it will happen, and it's often the founder's job to reverse this.

1. When was the last time you explored something new? If the answer is 'I cannot remember, then maybe you should lead from the front by experiencing what doing something new does to you.

Back in 2001, I took my entire Board of Directors skiing. None of them could ski. However, they all rose to the challenge. What happened to our numbers? We doubled turnover and tripled our profits the following year. Sometimes the best way to encourage an exploring mindset is to explore new things yourself.

Interestingly, one of the Group hated the experience and failed to progress. He was later in a great deal of trouble and was exited very expensively from the Group. May have been a coincidence?

Whether you are the explorer or the exploitation type, please keep firmly in mind that you need balance, and if you lose the balance, your business will fail.

Better still, always use an external advisor or two to remind you of this fact of life in business. Solving this issue alone will be worth the investment you make in your coach and Mastermind Group membership.

Balancing exploitation and exploration has a huge payoff and will ensure that your company stands the test of time.

If your business continues to balance these two elements, the business could still be trading in 100 years. If you fail to create the balance, your business may not survive next three years.

This section of how to grow your enterprise needs to be re-read every year.

Don't forget: after all, you are only human!

Exercise

Write down your thoughts on future-proofing your business to last 100 years or more.

32. Afterword

Congratulations on reading this book and taking the steps towards being the best entrepreneur you can be and financial freedom.

We also hope that this book will, in some small way, ensure that your business contributes to the world becoming a better place, for you to be able to make more money, gain more time freedom, have fun, and continually love what you do.

Our primary aim is to serve you our clients. To advise and support entrepreneurs to add value, grow, thrive, and have fun. If you wish to discuss how we could help you, then email me directly david.h@ thegrowthgurus.co.uk

Feel free to explore our website www.thegrowthgurus.co.uk and our Facebook Group; The Growth Gurus

We would welcome your stories and experiences in growing your business, both good and bad. We may even be able to help you find the answers to the challenges you face.

If you believe others would benefit from this book, send me their name, email, business name, and business address, and we will send you a discount code to use with Amazon.

Good luck out there, and remember, when you are an entrepreneur, walking the dog is included in your 'work time' no matter what you are thinking about!

If you wish to be included in our daily blog, register at www.thegrowthgurus.co.uk/blog

David Hugo Hargreaves

Walker of the family dogs, daddy to two beautiful girls, Writer of amazing blogs, thought leader extraordinaire, speaker, author, and not at all politically correct.

33. The Growth Gurus Development Programs

We offer a suite of outstanding training, mentoring, support and accountability to help you grow your business and build your wealth.

The main options for you;

1. Online training

2. Group training, accountability, and support

3. Mastermind Groups

4. One to one mentoring, accountability, and support

5. Bootcamps

To view these in detail, please visit our website www.thegrowthgurus. co.uk

1. Online training

We have a growing series of online courses that guide you through every aspect of growing your business.

2. Group mentoring, accountability, and support

We have a growing series of online mentoring, accountability and support sessions that guide you through every aspect of growing your business.

3. Mastermind Groups

Each month you will be joined by 8-10 of your peers for a 2 to 3-hour zoom meet-up.

You can then discuss your ideas and the challenges you face with other entrepreneurs. Your Peers can then offer their advice and hold you accountable for your objectives. Powerful stuff!

I will also be present during the Mastermind, and so you are also gaining 3 hours of access to me.

This valuable feedback and accountability will inevitably make you $/£ millions.

4. One to one mentoring, accountability, and support

For massive growth then choose my one-to-one face to face mentoring to ensure you reach your goals. We cover everything in this book and more, and that includes being held accountable

5. Bootcamps

Every quarter we hold a five-day book camp somewhere glamorous where we put you through your paces. Not only will I be attending, but so will a number of our Gurus to help you to master video, wealth building, sales strategies, marketing strategies, Linkedin, etc.

The boot camps are luxury retreats and only for those determined to own 7 figure businesses and be financially free as quickly as possible.

To access our mentoring support www.thegrowthgurus.co.uk/ mentor

- To access our online course **www.thegrowthgurus.co.uk/onlinecourse**

- To access the Mastermind Group **www.thegrowthgurus.co.uk/mastermind**

- To access our funding team **www.thegrowthgurus.co.uk/funding**

- To access our website team **www.thewebsitegurus.co.uk**

- To access the LinkedIn team **www.inlinked.co.uk**

Mission Critical Support that we offer to enhance your growth and wealth

We supply most of the resources that you will need to support you and your scaling enterprise.

We also have a world-class team of professionals who offer the following services that you can take advantage of;

1. Mentoring you and your team

2. Holding you accountable

3. Being your ally and supporter.

4. Finance or investment to fund your growth

5. Membership of one of our Mastermind Groups

6. Sales training.

7. Business buying training and ongoing support

8. Website design, development, and ongoing support

9. LinkedIn training, management, and ongoing support

10. Facebook training and management and ongoing support

11. Youtube training and management and ongoing support

12. Google training and management and ongoing support

13. Financial Management training and ongoing support

14. CRM design, implementation, and ongoing support

15. Mastering video presentation training

16. Access to our world-class accountants and heavily reduced rates.

17. Access to our Fractional Sales Director

18. Access to our Fractional Finance Director

19. Access to our Fractional HR Director

20. Access to our Fractional IT Director

21. Brand design and management

22. Digital advice, implementation, and ongoing support

23. HR advice, implementation, and ongoing support

24. Access to our M&A and Commercial solicitors

25. Export advice and support.

26. Cybersecurity

First published by David Hargreaves 2017

© 2017 by David Hargreaves

Print Book ISBN:

eBook ISBN

URGENT PLEA!

Thank You For Reading My Book!

I really appreciate all of your feedback, and I love hearing what you have to say.

I need your input to make the next version of this book and my future books better.

Please leave me a helpful review on Amazon letting me know what you thought of the book.

Thanks so much!!

- David Hugo Hargreaves

ABOUT THE AUTHOR

David Hargreaves is a college dropout who has, over the last 25 years, built several £multi million companies, including a prominent law firm, a niche insurance company, a pioneering claims management company, and an investment business.

David has been a Private Equity investor for several years, investing in established high-growth businesses that make a difference to people worldwide.

Over the last eight years, David has built The Growth Gurus to help others build their businesses quickly and sustainably while building their wealth and achieving financial freedom.

David is the founder of Investor Hub and Claritas Partners, two businesses that help High Net Worth clients constantly achieve high returns on their investments.

David is on a mission to help 1 million business founders to achieve financial freedom through his books, online training, mentorship programs, Mastermind Groups, and investment strategies.

David is also a dad to two wonderful girls who are just 5 and 8 at the time of writing, both of whom are likely to be business owners themselves.

Printed in Great Britain
by Amazon

85103903R00200